Dramas
with a
Message

VOLUME TWO

Books by Doug Fagerstrom

Baker Handbook of Single Adult Ministry (gen. ed.)
Counseling Single Adults (gen. ed.)
Dramas with a Message—Volume One
Dramas with a Message—Volume Two
Dramas with a Message—Volume Three
The Lonely Pew (with Jim Carlson)
Single Adult Ministry, the Second Step (gen. ed.)
Single to God (gen. ed.)
Single to Single (gen. ed.)
Singles Ministries Handbook (gen. ed.)
Worship and Drama Library, volume 15

Dramas
with a
Message

21 Reproducible Dramatic
Sketches for the Local Church

VOLUME TWO

DOUG FAGERSTROM

kregel
PUBLICATIONS

Grand Rapids, MI 49501

Dramas with a Message: 21 Reproducible Dramatic Sketches for the Local Church—Volume Two

© 1999 by Doug Fagerstrom

Published by Kregel Publications, a division of Kregel, Inc., P.O. Box 2607, Grand Rapids, MI 49501. Kregel Publications provides trusted, biblical publications for Christian growth and service. Your comments and suggestions are valued.

For more information about Kregel Publications, visit our web site: www.kregel.com

Cover photo: © PhotoDisc
Cover design: Nicholas G. Richardson
Book design: Kevin Ingram

Library of Congress Cataloging-in-Publication Data
Fagerstrom, Douglas L.
Dramas with a message: 21 reproducible dramatic sketches for the local church—volume one / Doug Fagerstrom.
    p.   cm.
  1. Drama in public worship. 2. Drama in Christian education. 3. Christian drama, American. I. Title.
BV289F34   1999   246'.72—dc21   99-43099
                                                CIP

ISBN 0-8254-2581-6 (v. 1)
ISBN 0-8254-2582-4 (v. 2)
ISBN 0-8254-2583-2 (v. 3)

Printed in the United States of America
1 2 3 4 5 / 03 02 01 00 99

A Note to the Drama Director

Dramas with a Message is designed for the worship service or special program in local churches or ministries. Sketches are short—about five to seven minutes in length. Stage set-up is simple, often needing only a chair, table, or hand props, and you are permitted to photocopy as many scripts as you need. Actors can be inexperienced, since the characters and lines come out of everyday events.

Some sketches are comical (although that is not their primary purpose), some are serious, and some have an ending that will surprise the audience. All of them carry simple themes. They are not complicated with hidden messages or deep theological truths. While the dramas can stand alone, they often work better as illustrations in a service or program. Not every sketch attempts to deliver an entire message. Some leave the audience "hanging" and in need of a speaker to complete the point. You, the director, will determine how best to fit a sketch into its context.

Know your audience. Know the message for the program. Know your actors. Select the right sketch—and then, have fun! Enjoy the sketches. Build a team of actors and support staff who will value being part of a ministry that delivers biblical principles and truths in an entertaining way.

Blessings as you share the message of Good News through these dramas.

DOUG FAGERSTROM

Acknowledgments

These sketch volumes are dedicated to the faithful actors and actresses at Calvary Church who volunteer their time and talent and have graciously performed these sketches at the "Saturday Night" ministry, each and every week.

Contents

The
Adam's
Family

THEME

We have all heard the story of Adam and Eve in the Garden. But, too often, we don't make the connection that their original sin is much like our sin each and every day. The enemy is real. The temptation is real. The sin and its consequences are real.

CHARACTERS

ADAM: Our first man, dressed in solid-colored sweats. He is a slob.

EVE: Our first woman, a perfectionist, dressed similar to Adam.

SG: "Some Guy," represents the Devil. He is dressed in a flashy checked/plaid sport coat and carries a briefcase containing a brush, a booklet, lipstick, a frying pan, and a large red apple with a large price tag attached. He is a huckster.

NARRATOR: Can be a male or a female voice.

SETTING

A very messy living room and kitchen table. Clothes and empty food containers are thrown everywhere. A chair for Eve is near the table, stage right. A couch is stage left. A newspaper, chips, a door, and a doorbell are needed for props.

Adam is sleeping on the couch. Snoring is appropriate.

NARRATOR: So the Lord God caused the first man, Adam, to fall into a deep sleep; and while he was sleeping, he took one of the man's ribs. Then the Lord God made a woman from the rib he had taken and brought the woman to the man.

[Eve walks in and sits in the chair and stares at the audience with no expression.]

ADAM: *[wakes up, yawns, stretches, and rubs his side]* Oh, my aching side. *[pause]* I had the strangest dream last night. . . . *[keeps rubbing side]* Boy, this couch has got to go. My side is killing me. It must have been that pizza or those ribs I ate last night. *[looks up]* Ah, God, I'm trying to tell you, this single life is not for me. I sure wish you would listen to me. Now, where did I put the pepto? *[searches around and sees Eve]* Wow! Badda-boom, badda-bing! *What* are you?!

EVE: *[coyly with some assertiveness]* I *am* a woman!

ADAM: Great! And *what* is a wo-man?

EVE: *[exasperated]* Oh, brother, why did I know this was going to happen? I guess I am just going to have to explain everything to you. *[short pause]* Ah, are you any relation to Fred Flintstone? You know, you remind me a lot of—

ADAM: By the way, what are you doing here? *[he leans over]* Did, ah, . . . He *[points up]* send you?

EVE: *[flirtatiously]* Yes, and what do you think?

ADAM: I have been making a few requests about the single life and, well, *[looks her over]* you do beat a rhino or one of those hippopotamuses.

EVE: *[sarcastically]* That is the nicest compliment I have ever had . . . *[under her breath]* since it is the only one.

ADAM: Hey . . . ah, cute stuff, . . . are you into climbing trees?

EVE: Look, mister, I could do a lot for you!

ADAM: *[skeptical]* Yeah? Like what?

[Adam sits down on couch and begins to feed his face with chips and tunes out with a newspaper.]

EVE: *[taking charge]* First of all, I can teach you how to clean up after yourself. *[picks up junk, looks rather disheartened]* Then again? . . . I can teach you a lot about life! I can help you make a few better choices than the ones you have already made. For instance, I think we need to . . . Have you heard anything I have said?

[doorbell rings]

ADAM: *[looks up from paper]* Sure, babe, haven't missed a beat. . . . And you can begin by answering the door.

[Eve reluctantly opens the door.]

SG: Adam's family? Say, I was just passing through the neighborhood and thought I would see if I could be of some help to you and the hubby. I have a *fine* line of personal care and home improvement products.

EVE: *[desperately]* I am open to anything. You would not believe what I have to work with. Life for me is less than two hours old, and I have been delt a bad hand.

SG: *[looks at Adam]* Hey, I think I know what you mean, but I can fix you up, no problem.

EVE: So, what do you have?

SG: First of all, I have a great line of Fuller Brushes. *[shows her a brush and a booklet]*

EVE: I'll take them all!

SG: Great! Now, have you heard about . . . Amway? I think that you would make a great distributor, and for only the small amount of—

EVE: *[leans over to SG]* Will this Amway get me out of the house?

SG: Of course!

EVE: Sign me up!

SG: Now, I think a few Mary Kay Cosmetics would be right up your alley. *[holds out a tube of lipstick]*

EVE: What are cosmetics?

SG: Whoa, you don't get out much, do you? Makeup, lady, makeup! These little wonders will put magic into your man for those special moments when . . . *[Both stare at Adam as he is sitting with his feet on couch, reading the paper, and shoveling food into his mouth.]* . . . the two of . . . you . . . *[SG and Eve look at each other.]*

EVE/SG: Not!

SG: How about some cooking utensils? *[offers a small pan]*

EVE: *[examines item as a potential weapon, and reconsiders]* No thanks.

SG: I know, I have just the thing for you. *[pulls out a large red apple, with a large price tag on it]*

EVE: *[skeptical]* And *what* is that?

SG: Why, it is the most wonderful, most powerful thing you have ever seen or heard of.

EVE: Will it slice and dice?

SG: It will change your life!

EVE: Yeah? How so?

SG: Lady, this will put you right at the top. You will be the envy of . . . well . . .

envy itself! Think of it! Power, fame, fortune, your name in lights. You can have it all!

EVE: How can I believe you?

SG: Hey, do I look like a liar? Honesty is my business. The Big Guy Upstairs knows who I am. In fact, He is on my résumé. He has called me a prince and an angel of light. Now, you don't see Him stopping me, do you? So, what could be so wrong? The choice is entirely yours!

EVE: *[looks at large price tag on apple]* Oh, I don't know. It looks kind of expensive. In fact, this could cost a lot. *[looks over to Adam]* Adam, what do you think?

ADAM: *[responds with mouth full, looks over his newspaper]* Anything you say, babe. Checkbook is somewhere on the table. See if he'll take a postdated check.

SG: *[smooth]* Hey, no problem. My policy is buy now and pay later . . . even if it is much later. Don't worry.

EVE: Okay, I'll take one. You know, I could not have done this without you. You have really helped me a lot. Besides, it's not like we are going to fall over dead or something.

[SG responds with nervous laugh and leaves. Eve sits in chair admiring the apple.]

ADAM: Hey, wo-man. Who was the little guy with the funny clothes?

EVE: I don't know. Just some guy. At least he wasn't pushy. *[pause]* Adam, did you hear what he said about a new life, fame, fortune, and all that other stuff?

ADAM: Sorry, babe, I wasn't paying much attention. It's not my job. I figure you can take care of the domestic stuff.

EVE: You just aren't going to be of any help, are you? *[confident]* Well, I made a choice, and I am going to stick with it, and I don't care what you say, even if you were the last man on earth. *[She cuts apple in half and puts it on a plate for Adam.]*

ADAM: *[delighted]* What a woman . . . knows how to get to a guy's heart . . . through his—*[stands, begins to rub stomach, then rubs side]* boy my side is really killing me.

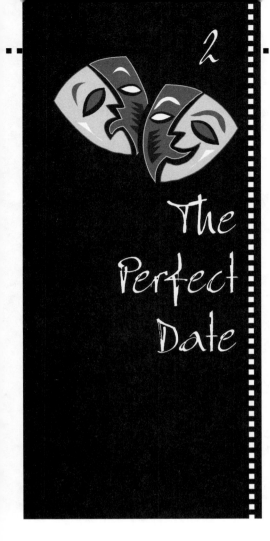

THEME

What appears to be success in one's own eyes can really be total failure in the eyes of another. Our own perceptions are not always the truth in winning or losing.

CHARACTERS

LEROY: A person who tries hard in life. His insecurity and false/obnoxious view of himself attracts judgmental responses from others. There is no doubt that he thinks of himself as a "winner." He cannot grasp that he is really losing, big time. His hair is greased back, and he wears out-of-style clothing.

ANGELA: She has it all together. She was kind enough to go on a date with LeRoy but would never attempt a second date. It was an awful experience. She doesn't mince words sharing "the rest of the story."

SETTING

Stage right and stage left each have an easy chair, end table, and phone.

LeRoy and Angela are each on the phone reporting to a friend their big date. Each one freezes at the end of his or her line, while one character picks up instantly on the keyword *from the other.*

LEROY: *[dials phone]* Ernie? *[pause]* Oh, I'm sorry; may I talk to Ernie? Sure, I can wait. *[while waiting, sings a romantic song]* Hey, Ernie; yeah, LeRoy here. . . . You will not guess what happened last night. Old fox here had the date of his life. Yes, it was Angela. *[macho voice]* I mean, my little Angel. It was the *night* of nights.

ANGELA: *[talks on phone] Nightmare!* Ruthie, it was a nightmare! That frog belched after every dinner course, and he kept calling me Angel—couldn't even get my name right. And his *clothes* . . .

LEROY: Ernie, I *looked* great, and let me tell you, I went a little extra and bought her the best roses money could buy. You would have been *proud* of me.

ANGELA: What a *proud*, arrogant pinhead. I was humiliated. The macho mess shows up a half-hour late wearing his leisure suit, carrying a long stem *mum*—and the ugly thing is plastic—*[pause]* no Ruthie, the *mum* was plastic.

13

LeRoy: *[dreamy]* She was gorgeous, and just like in the movies, we sped off with the top down into the sunset and for the best night of my *life*.

Angela: I thought my *life* was over. It was like a horror movie. It rained all night and his after-market sunroof leaked all over my white slacks . . . and the guy drives so fast, we got a speeding ticket before we even got to the *free*way.

LeRoy: Ernie, I spared no expense. We did it right! We went to the 1915 Room and ordered the best! Let me tell you, it was worth the extra bucks for my Angel. The night was just too *short*.

Angela: *Short*, the guy was short twenty bucks. If I hadn't just cashed my check, I would still be doing dishes at Ponderosa with old frog-breath.

LeRoy: Heh, heh, my manual for successful dating should be in the bookstores any day. Oh, how sweet it is, Ernie! What a way to *live*.

Angela: *Die*, Ruthie, I thought I was going to die. There we were, seated by the window right next to the hot food buffet, and the ying yang starts playing with the candle. He drips wax all over the table, the kids next to us are staring, their parents are laughing, and then he lights the napkin on fire, and the guy on the other side throws a glass of water at us, misses the burning napkin, and douses the turkey's tie-dyed madras shirt. Oh, Ruthie, how can I ever forget last *night*.

LeRoy: It was a *night* to remember. It ended fantastic. We went for a long, romantic walk and—*[interrupted]* What? What time did we get back? You're pushing me for the good stuff, aren't you, Ernie. All right, all right, if you have to have the truth, it was *midnight*.

Angela: *One A.M.*, the jerk brings me home at one A.M. I thought he was pulling a fast one on me with the old "run out of gas" routine. Ruthie, he *did* run out of gas! And I had to walk to the service station, pay the five dollar gas can deposit, and walk back—in the rain.

LeRoy: I can't wait to see her *again*.

Angela: If I ever see that flea-brain *again* . . .

LeRoy: I'll give her some time and call in a *week*.

Angela: I will send him into next *week* if he knocks on my door.

LeRoy: Yes, Ernie, I'm a *winner*.

Angela: You said it Ruthie, he is a *loser*.

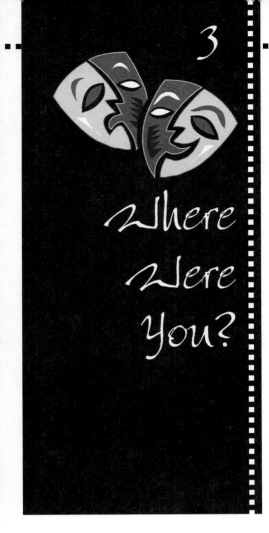

3

Where Were You?

THEME

We all sin. When we do, we feel the guilt that either draws us closer to God with confession and repentance or away from God with failure and despair. Sometimes we feel that God has abandoned us, when we are the ones who have walked away.

CHARACTERS

JANICE: Dressed casually with an overcoat and suitcase.

MAN IN CHAIR: Represents Jesus.

SETTING

Man is sitting in a high-backed chair with back to audience at stage center. The audience never sees his face. A small end table and another chair or couch faces the high-backed chair, positioned so the audience can see the character seated in the chair/couch.

SCENE 1

Janice is sitting on chair/couch, with coat on, suitcase beside her, ready to leave. Man is sitting in chair.

JANICE: *[very upset]* I have had it with You! You just sit there! I never hear a word out of You. And You don't do anything! How many times have I asked for Your help? How many? See, You don't say a word. You expect me to read Your mind. Well, I am sorry, I am not a mind reader. *[She begins to get up.]* You don't leave me any choice. I'm leaving! I've had it. *[She moves forward, most of the way, but hesitates as if she wants Him to come after her.]* Did You hear me? I am out of here. History. Gone! All right, all right . . . but don't say I didn't warn You . . . or give You a chance. *[She gets up and looks/speaks to audience.]* And what are you staring at? *[points back to man in chair]* He is all yours. Maybe you can do something with that . . . that rock! God knows I have done everything possible. *[down in aisle now]* Oh yeah, welcome to _____ *[insert name of your program]*, but I'm leaving! *[She exits.]*

SCENE 2

Janice comes walking up center aisle carrying her suitcase. She appears exhausted. She meanders onto the platform and throws her suitcase on the floor, sits in the chair/couch, and is startled when she sees that the man is sitting in the chair.

JANICE: *[startled, amazed]* Whoa! What are You doing here?

MAN: *[kind and strong]* What do you mean? I do live here, or did you forget?

JANICE: No, but I really didn't expect to see You . . . here.

MAN: But I promised that I would not leave . . . no matter what you said . . . or did.

JANICE: I guess after the way I acted and, well, after our last time together, it seemed pretty obvious that You . . . You would—

MAN: *[kind and firm]* Leave you? Not a chance. How many times did I tell you that I love you?

JANICE: Love me? Like a broken record, but I also told You that I wasn't sure about my commitment to You. *[more intense/blaming]* I didn't always feel like You were listening to me. Half the time You never responded. *[irritated]* I sometimes feel like I am just talking to a brick wall.

MAN: *[sincere]* I'm sorry you felt that way. I never wanted to hurt you. I hope you believe me when I say that.

JANICE: *[a bit reluctant]* Sure, but there were times when the things You said to me hurt, and You sure know how to make me feel guilty. I'm not perfect, even though I know You—

MAN: Look, I'm not keeping score. And I know what it is to have someone you love walk out on you. You're right, it does hurt. *[pause]* I am glad you are finally home. Can we start over now?

JANICE: *[with great desire]* I want to, I really do. *[shameful]* But, I did some pretty awful things while I was gone. I'm not sure I can ever look You in the face again. I am so ashamed.

MAN: *[calm]* Janice, I know what you have done.

JANICE: *[surprised]* You what?

MAN: I know everything.

JANICE: *[wondering]* How could You? I made sure that no one knew where I was going. *[thinks]* That Betty! I knew I should never have confided in her. Why, I will ring her ever loving—

MAN: Janice, it wasn't Betty, even though she did let you down.

JANICE: Then, how did You know?

MAN: Let's just say I have my ways of finding things out.

JANICE: *[embarrassed]* Then You know about . . .

MAN: Yes, Janice.

JANICE: And . . .

MAN: That too.

JANICE: Then I guess I might as well go. . . . *[gets up, begins to pick up coat to leave]*

MAN: Wait, Janice. Sit down and take my hand. *[He reaches out his hand to hers; she slowly responds by giving her hand.]* I love you. I always will.

JANICE: *[passionate]* Lord, I love You too. And please forgive me for leaving You and going my own way. Help me, Jesus, please help me. A—

MAN: Wait, don't finish with "Amen." We are not done. Don't close off our time together, because it is forever. Janice, I do forgive you . . . for everything. So you don't need to leave this time, okay?

JANICE: Okay, Lord. I really do love You!

Optional Scripture reading of Hebrews 13:4-6: [Offstage voice reads as characters freeze.] "Marriage should be honored by all, for God will judge the adulterer and all the sexually immoral. Keep your lives free from the love of money and be content with what you have, because the Lord has said, 'Never will I leave you; never will I forsake you.' So, we say with confidence, 'The Lord is my helper, I will not be afraid.'"

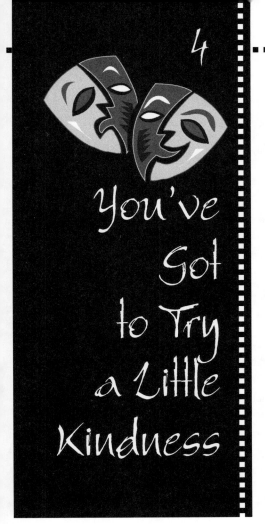

4

You've Got to Try a Little Kindness

THEME

When life is tough and people are difficult, it is almost impossible to respond with love and kindness. Yet, God has given us the fruit of His Spirit, kindness, for every difficult encounter.

CHARACTERS

BILL: Bonnie's ex-husband. He is dressed very casually.

BONNIE: A single parent of three children. She is dressed extremely casually.

VOICE: Represents God (scene 4 only).

SETTING

Living room with a door (if possible), couch, phone, and end table.

Director's Note: The four scenes may run consecutively or separately. If separate, Bonnie could do a simple change of clothes. It is nice if some music bridges the various scenes.

SCENE 1

Bonnie comes into the living room with a stack of mail in her hand. She sits on the couch.

BONNIE: *[opens a letter, upset]* Oh, great! *[reads]* We wish to inform you that your phone will be disconnected unless we receive the past due amount in our office before October 17. *[looks up]* The seventeenth?! That's today. *[angry]* Wait until I get my hands on that ex-husband of mine. Why, I'm going to ring his—*[phone rings]* Well, it still works. *[picks up phone, angry voice]* This is Bonnie! Oh, hi Jan. I'm surprised you got through. *[pause]* Oh, Billy boy did it again. Yes, he didn't pay the phone bill, so now service is going to be cut off. *[pause]* But I don't have the $47.93 to run down there and pay it. Besides, I have bailed him out for the last time, and I am not going to cover his . . . Jan? Jan?

[blackout]

SCENE 2

This is another time of the day. Bonnie has gone through the mail, which is now on the floor, and she is trying to read a book. She is obviously not focused on the book.

BONNIE: *[sitting on couch trying to read, keeps looking at watch, speaks with anger]* Twenty minutes late. Why am I always the one waiting? Just once I wish he would show me a little respect. But he is the most inconsiderate human being that was ever hatched on this planet! I'm going to give him a piece of my—*[knock at the door, Bonnie goes to open the door, but stops short and says with vengeance:]* This man has no idea what he is walking into. *[She freezes.]*

BILL: *[standing at door thinking of excuses why he is late . . . again]* I'll bet she is hotter than hot. Last time I was only eleven and a half minutes late, and I am still paying for that one. *[rubs jaw]* This is going to be World War III. *[rehearsing excuses]* Let's see, ah, the car broke down. No, used that last time. I know, I lost my keys. No, used that one last month. *[deep sigh]* Yes! I was a witness to an accident, and I had to stop and report to the police everything that I saw. Good one, Bill! Yes, Bill wins again! *[knocks on door again; Bonnie comes back to life]*

BONNIE: *[opens door]* Look, you don't have to break the door down, I heard you the first time.

BILL: *[stutters in fear as he tries to be convincing]* I . . . I, ah, . . . saw an accident at 3rd and Pine, you know, where 3rd Street crosses Pine, and this car hit this . . . *[becomes very dramatic]* ah, pole . . . and this guy was standing by the pole, and the pole fell over, and the guy ran out in the street, and another car swerved, and my car was in the turn lane, and the truck, yeah, this big truck came out of the corner . . . the corner of my eye and ran over the man . . . hole cover that was in the center. And so I had to stay and tell the police everything that happened. And so that is why I am just a couple of minutes—

BONNIE: *[claps her hands, cynical]* That was good. You should win an academy award, you two-faced, lying, no good bum! You didn't see an accident any more than you saw a pink elephant.

BILL: *[no emotion]* Look, here's your money. *[hands her a stack of bills]* That's all you want anyway, so just take it, and I'm out of here. *[begins to leave]*

BONNIE: *[quickly counts bills]* Wait, Mr. Eyewitness. This is only half of it. Where is the rest? How am I supposed to feed *your* kids and get by on this? And what about the phone bill? *[He turns and begins walking away.]* Yeah, just walk away. That is what you always do, Bill. Just walk away. Every time you come, it's the same. You haven't changed, and you never will. I hope you are a witness to an accident, Bill, [screaming] yours!

[blackout]

SCENE 3

This scene is clearly another day. A sign may be held up to the audience, "Another Day."

BONNIE: [sitting on couch trying to read a book, keeps looking at watch, speaks with bitterness] Twenty-five minutes late. Why am I always the one waiting? Just once I wish he would show me a little respect. But he is the most inconsiderate human being that was ever . . . discovered. I am going to give him a little of his own medicine. [knocks on door; Bonnie goes to open the door; again, she freezes on the way]

BILL: [standing at door thinking of excuses why he is late . . . again] I'll bet she is hotter than a butane torch. Last time I was only twenty minutes late, and I am still paying for that one [rubs ears]. This is going to be nuclear war. Let's see . . . [pulls out a three by five card] ah, car broke, no, ah, lost keys, witness to accident, nooooo, used that one last time. [deep sigh] Yes! I was in an accident! Good one, Bill! Yes, Bill wins again! [knocks on door; Bonnie comes back to life]

BONNIE: [opens door, speaks sarcastically] Hello, Bill, did you lose your keys again, or was it another accident you saw?

BILL: I was in an accident, Bonnie. It was horrible.

BONNIE: [cynical] I am sure it was. You poor thing. Why, you look all beaten up. How can I add to your . . . I mean, can I help you with anything?

BILL: [humbled] You aren't buying this one bit, are you, Bonnie?

BONNIE: [cynical] Why, Bill, what would make you say a thing like that?

BILL: [honest for the first time] Because we have never been really honest with each other since we were married, so it is a little hard for me to buy into all this sugarcoated—

BONNIE: Bill, Bill, Bill, you just can't figure things out, can you? Or would you rather have me tearing your pointed little head off and knocking some sense into your thick—

BILL: That would make more sense than this. *[hands her the money]* Here, Bonnie, I hope this helps a little.

BONNIE: *[shuts door and counts money, yells]* Fifty short! Why that no good, two-timing, two-faced phony!

[blackout]

SCENE 4

In this final scene, a little kindness is shown, finding that it really is the best way, God's way, to handle conflict. A sign may be shown to the audience, "Another Day" or "Another Day, Again."

BONNIE: *[sitting on couch trying to read a book, keeps looking at watch, speaks with deep hurt]* Thirty minutes late. Why am I always the one waiting? Just once I wish he would show me a little respect. But he is the most inconsiderate human being that was ever hatched in a test tube. *[anger rises]* No more Miss Nice Lady. This is the final chapter—*[knock on door; she gets up and freezes when she hears the voice]*

VOICE: Be kind, compassionate, forgiving, as Christ forgave you! And the fruit of the Spirit is kindness.

BILL: *[standing at door thinking of excuses why he is late . . . again]* I'll bet she is hotter than a Bunsen burner. Last time I was only twenty-five minutes late. This is going to be like the home of _____. *[Identify a current villain in life.]* Let's see . . . *[pulls out a long sheet of paper]* ah, car broke, lost keys, witness to accident, in accident. . . . The truth. Hm, haven't tried that one. Okay, the truth. *[freezes]*

BONNIE: *[comes to life and goes to open the door, stops, and looks up to God]* Look, God, I heard what you just said, and you make the kindness thing sound so simple, but let me tell you, it isn't. But right now I have nothing to lose . . . so, here goes. *[opens door, speaks sincerely, but it is obvious that she is struggling]* Hello, Bill, how are you?

BILL: Bonnie, I'm sorry I'm late, you see, it was my—

BONNIE: Bill, save it. It's okay. I just want us to be able to get along.

BILL: *[surprised]* Say what? Bonnie, really, the reason that I wasn't here on time—

BONNIE: Bill . . . *[She puts her hand up as a truce sign and to quiet him.]* it doesn't matter.

BILL: *[curious]* It doesn't?

BONNIE: No, there are more important things than you or me winning these little battles. The kids are far more important, and what is happening to us is . . . very important. So, if we can at least just be *[looks up to God]* kind, I think it can go a long way to make things better.

BILL: *[hands over money]* Here, Bonnie. *[turns to walk away, but stops and reaches in pocket and pulls out some more money and, just as he turns to give her the rest, the door shuts and Bill is left standing and says:]* Bonnie, here's the rest!

[blackout]

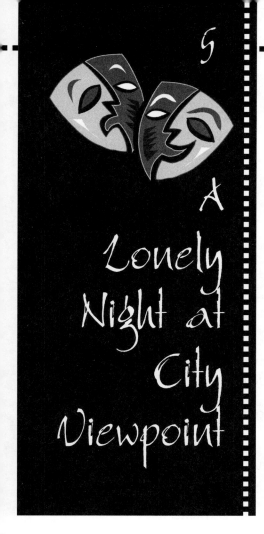

5

A Lonely Night at City Viewpoint

THEME

Skip Skipper, a radio talk show host, thinks he has all the answers to the issue of loneliness, until a five-year-old tells him differently.

CHARACTERS

SKIP SKIPPER: A late-night radio talk show host. He is smooth, cool, suave, and arrogant. He is dressed casually in contemporary clothes.

The following are voices only:

LENNY: A regular nightly call-in. He comes off as obnoxious but is obviously lonely and just tries too hard.

JANE: A stereotypical lonely person. She is in search of anyone who will listen to her.

ANDY: A five-year-old child. He is a little nervous and timid but seems to have a better handle on life than the talk show host.

SETTING

The stage is a sound studio set with a wild array of electronic components, microphones, and telephones for our host, Skip Skipper.

SKIP: *[musical theme ends]* Oh yeah! That makes four weeks and running in the number one spot! And you're listening to 92.5 on your dial where the talk is the best. And it's time again for "City Viewpoint." I am your host, Skip Skipper! Yes, it is yours truly and truly yours, the brains, the mind, the legend of our time, with grace and finesse, I am the best. You have the questions, Skip has the answers. So pick up that phone and give me a call right here at 555-9000. And our first caller . . . Hello, caller, you're on the air.

LENNY: *[enthusiastically]* Uh, hi Skip, this is Lenny, remember me? I'm your best friend, buddy.

SKIP: *[skeptically]* Yeah, Lenny, it's great to have you call . . . again. So, what can I do for you tonight, Lenny?

LENNY: Well, Skip, I was wondering what there is to do on a _____ *[insert night of your program]*. I am feeling a little . . . you know, after working in the shop all day and all, I was just wondering if you and some of the guys would like to join me and—

SKIP: Lenny, my man, the malls are still open, take a walk. *[clicks a button on his phone]* Next caller, you're on the air.

JANE: *[timid]* Hello?

SKIP: Hello?

JANE: Hello? Am I on the air?

SKIP: Hello! You're on the air.

JANE: I don't think I'm on the air. Should I call back and try again?

SKIP: Good idea. . . . *[click]* City Viewpoint, you are on the air.

LENNY: Hi Skip, it's Lenny. By the way, which mall would you recommend I go to? There are several, and I would really appreciate your advice.

SKIP: The Mall of America in Minneapolis. Try that one, Lenny.

LENNY: Great, Skip, I'll come by the station and pick you up. None of the guys were . . . available to go with me, and since you're my best friend, I just thought you and me—

SKIP: *[click]* City Viewpoint. This is where the talk . . . is . . . best!

JANE: Hello, Skip? This is Jane, and I called back. Can you hear me?

SKIP: I can hear you, Jane, what is your question?

JANE: Well, I was wondering how I could make some friends.

SKIP: You have to get out, Jane. Have you tried the mall?

JANE: Every day, but that's a pretty lonely place, Skip.

SKIP: Well, Jane, you just have to work a little harder at it. How about having some folks over to your place, you know, a little party-time?

JANE: But I don't know who to call.

SKIP: Jane, Jane, finding friends is easy. You just have to be bold, make up your mind that you are not going to be lonely, and change your environment.

JANE: That's it?

SKIP: Simple as that.

JANE: *[with great hesitation]* Well, would you like to come over with some of your friends? I'll buy the Doritos!

SKIP: *[click]* Next caller, you're on the air.

ANDY: *[amazed]* Wow, is this Mr. Skipper?

SKIP: Yours truly and truly yours.

ANDY: Hi, my name is Andy, and I am five years old.

SKIP: Well, Andy, aren't you up a little late?

ANDY: Nope, I got this new radio for my birthday, and I heard you say that finding friends is easy, and my mom and dad are gone again, . . . and I'm kind of home alone, and I was just wondering if you would be my new friend.

SKIP: *[playing along]* Sure, Andy, I will be your new friend. Let's play a game and pretend that I am a football player and you are—

ANDY: Mr. Skip . . . per, I thought that friends didn't have to pretend and play games. I thought that friends could be real people, so I thought maybe you could come over and play Legos at my house.

SKIP: *[tongue-tied, isn't sure what to say to a five-year-old]* Legos. Okay? Andy, buddy, don't you have some friends your own age?

ANDY: That's okay, Mr. Skipper. I can tell that your voice sounds like my dad's when he is too busy to play with me. You don't have to be my friend. I just thought you sounded like a nice dad-kinda-guy and well . . . good-bye.

SKIP: Hey, Andy, hang on. I like . . . Legos and maybe . . .

[click; dial tone]

6

The Physical Exam

THEME

We all go to the doctor for physical exams. Well, Dr. Probe goes deeper as an eye, ear, nose, and tongue specialist. He definitely goes after the tongue with Waldo Moody. Waldo discovers a disease that is very serious.

CHARACTERS

DR. PROBE: An old-fashioned doctor, who lacks good "bedside manners." He speaks with a thick European accent.

WALDO MOODY: A lighthearted but rather loud, obnoxious person, whose internal maladies are many.

SETTING

A simple doctor's office with an examination stool and tools, a table for the patient to sit on, and an eye/word chart.

Dr. Probe and Waldo are in place. Dr. Probe is thoroughly examining Waldo without much TLC or concern for his patient's feelings. The doctor's comments are basically good on each area of examination, until he looks at Waldo's tongue.

WALDO: *[as Dr. Probe taps his leg with a hammer]* Ouch! That hurt!

DR. PROBE: Mr. Moody, you are going to have to cooperate with this examination if I am going to find out what is wrong with you! *[takes stethoscope, flashlight, etc., to continue exam]* So, would you please be quiet. *[begins to use stethoscope on chest]*

WALDO: *[laughs]* Doc, I'm ticklish. Please stop that!

DR. PROBE: And would you stop making all this noise. Goodness, you are worse than the children. *[mumbles with obvious disgust as he continues the exam]*

WALDO: *[looks bored as doctor exams his ear]* Hey, Doc, did you hear about the salesman who went door-to-door trying to sell—

DR. PROBE: Mr. Waldo Moody, would you please refrain from all of this babble. I am trying to help you.

WALDO: *[lighthearted]* Hey, relax Doc. I can take a hint. . . . *[starts whistling]* Doc, you would not believe what I heard seventh-hand about old Ms. Palmer. Why, let me tell you about that old—

DR. PROBE: Waldo!

WALDO: Yeah, Doc?

DR. PROBE: Stick a sock in it.

WALDO: Ooooo Doc, you're a bit testy. Maybe you should—

DR. PROBE: *[as Doc is examining Waldo's tongue with tongs and gauze]* Oh, Mr. Moody. Oh my . . . no, no, no . . . ah, ah, ah, this is not good. In fact, this is . . . Mr. Moody, how long have you been . . . living?

WALDO: *[with stuff still in mouth, alarmed]* Doc, what is it, what's wrong?

DR. PROBE: *[with genuine concern]* Mr. Moody, I have never seen anything so awful in all my days of medicine. I believe that you have a disease that is . . . incurable.

WALDO: *[panics]* Doc, what it is? What's wrong? Do I have that, you know, . . . do I have IT? Look, Doc, I have been mono . . . you know, monochrome or a mongrel since the first of the year, so it can't be—

DR. PROBE: Relax, Mr. Moody, you do not have that.

WALDO: Then . . . what is it, Doc? Give it to me straight.

DR. PROBE: I'll do my best. Mr. Waldo Moody, you have "hoof'n-mouth'n-pro-fanitis."

WALDO: Huh? What is that?

DR. PROBE: Well, can you spell hoof and mouth?

WALDO: So, what do I do about that, Doc? Is there something that I can take to get rid of it? You know, pills, shots, therapy?

DR. PROBE: Tell me, did your mother or father ever try soap in your mouth?

WALDO: Huh?

DR. PROBE: I am afraid, Mr. Moody, there is nothing that I can do to help you.

WALDO: So how long do I have, Doc?

DR. PROBE: How many friends do you have left?

WALDO: *[stumbles through a list of former friends]* Well, there is . . . no, ah . . . and there is, no, I guess she doesn't count anymore, . . . but there is, no, that jerk couldn't keep two pencils in a pocket protector straight. Hey, Doc, what's the point? Is this disease contagious?

DR. PROBE: Well, it can be, but the biggest problem is that a bad mouth is worse than bad breath because it drives everyone away.

WALDO: Look, Doc, you must be able to do something.

DR. PROBE: Well, we could sew your tongue to your teeth or staple your lips shut, but that would not get the ugly, nasty words out of your mind.

WALDO: I guess I'm a goner, huh, Doc?

DR. PROBE: It is easier to tame lions and tigers, Waldo.

WALDO: No one has made it, Doc?

DR. PROBE: Sorry, Mr. Moody.

WALDO: Well, God, I guess this one is up to you.

DR. PROBE: Wait a minute. *[looks into Waldo's mouth]* Say that again.

WALDO: Say what?

DR. PROBE: What you just said.

WALDO: *[more thoughtfully]* Well, God, I guess this one is up to you.

DR. PROBE: *[excited]* Mr. Moody, I think there is hope for you!

[blackout]

THEME

Eternal life/salvation is a free gift from God to us. Yet it was not free to God. The price was God's Son. No earthly gift or exchange can compare.

CHARACTERS

NATE WHEELER: A high-powered salesman. His dress is very flashy.

WILMA: Represents every person. She is dressed casually.

BETTY: A cynical skeptic. She is dressed semi-casually.

ALICE: A kind but curious doubter. She is dressed casually.

LUCILLE: An interested seeker. She is dressed very casually.

DOCTOR SPECK: Honest and to the point. He is wearing a white coat and tie or a suit.

SETTING

Stage settings are listed at the beginning of each scene.

Director's Note: The following three scenes can be done separately or run consecutively without breaks, moving from one stage set to the next.

SCENE 1

Setting: A small stand with a sign reading, "Eternal Life . . . Sale" is stage center. Nate Wheeler is standing behind the stand as Wilma approaches reading a newspaper.

NATE: *[loudly]* Welcome to our annual sale of Eternal Life. Step right up here, ma'am. How can I help you?

WILMA: *[timidly]* Well, I was just reading your ad here in the obituary section, and I was wondering about purchasing some Eternal Life.

NATE: Shop no more! You have found the fountain of the future, the happy hope, a heavenly home, and a guaranteed glory.

WILMA: And just how much is this going to cost?

NATE: *[waves a small rolled up paper with a ribbon on it]* Cost? Why, it won't hardly cost you anything when you consider the hope and joy that this little contract will bring to you and your loved ones.

WILMA: Okay, how much?

NATE: Just 3 percent of your income, and three hundred hours of community service. Why, you just need to shout thirty *Hallelujahs* and promise that you will join the church choir of your choice and bring your favorite dish to the next potluck dinner. *[softly]* And my little fee . . . *[points]* right here at the bottom.

WILMA: That's it?

NATE: That's it! We used to sell these little contracts for a whole lot more, but times have changed. People just aren't as interested. But, if you buy today, we will throw in seven years of good luck.

WILMA: *[with some hesitation]* What's the guarantee?

NATE: Guarantee? Think it through! Do you know anyone else in town who is offering as good a deal on Eternal Life? The hospital isn't offering *any* guarantees. Think about it! Has the IRS given any hope of Eternal Life? And our price is a whole lot better than that church around the corner. So, there you have it. Our product is as good as your money.

WILMA: *[looks at contract]* What is this fine print on the bottom?

NATE: *[a bit flustered]* Fine print? Ah, . . . just a little bit of the heavenly language, you know, Greek and Hebrew. It's just there to make the contract look a little more . . . official. You know, "Eternal Life talk." Makes everyone feel a whole lot better.

WILMA: *[rather nervous]* Oh . . . I don't know. . . . *[decisive]* Okay, I'll take one!

NATE: Fine choice. Now just sign here. *[Wilma signs.]* There, would you like it gift wrapped?

WILMA: No, I'll just take it like it is. Thanks. *[hands him money]*

NATE: And happily ever after. *[puts money into pocket]*

SCENE 2

Setting: Wilma is standing at the corner bus stop. Betty, Alice, and Lucille each walk past and stop to talk to Wilma.

BETTY: Wilma, how are you? I haven't seen you in—

WILMA: *[enthusiastically interrupts]* Betty, I am wonderful!

BETTY: Tell me what is so wonderful.

WILMA: I just got Eternal Life!

BETTY: Say what?

WILMA: Eternal Life! You know, the hereafter! Well, I am going to the hereafter!

BETTY: After what?

WILMA: Die, Betty, after we die! We are all going to die, Betty. And I just wanted to be sure what was going to happen. *[waving her contract]* But now I have the guarantee. I have hope.

BETTY: *[skeptical]* Wilma, no one can give you hope about life after death . . . especially that heaven stuff. Look, no one has been there and come back to prove it. I hope you didn't have to pay too much for that piece of . . . wallpaper. *[walking away]* Well, *good luck*, Wilma, you're going to need it.

WILMA: *[scrambles through her contract]* Good luck? Hey, I have that too . . . for seven years. *[Wilma appears doubtful.]*

ALICE: *[walking by]* Hi, Wilma. Nice day isn't it?

WILMA: *[downcast]* Oh, hi, Alice.

ALICE: Whoa, you look like you just lost your last friend.

WILMA: Alice, do you believe in the hereafter?

ALICE: Yeah, I think so. If not, life is just a cruel joke.

WILMA: *[waving contract]* What would you say if I told you that I have a guaranteed contract for Eternal Life?

ALICE: Wilma, I would say you have lost it and it is time to give the men with white coats your address.

WILMA: Well, I have a guarantee. *[Lucille walks up.]* Hey, Lucille, what do you think?

LUCILLE: What do I think about what?

ALICE: Wilma has this harebrained idea that you can guarantee life in the hereafter.

LUCILLE: I did see a movie one time about people going to heaven, or was that Cincinnati? I can't remember. But heaven sounds nice. *[upset tone of voice]* But do I have to live next door to the same neighbors, because if I do . . .

ALICE: Wilma, just admit it. You got ripped off. There are no guarantees. I hope you can get your money back. Come on, Lucille, we're going to be late for the matinee. *[They begin exiting.]*

LUCILLE: You know, I'm not too excited about the hereafter. Do you think we will have to fly like angels? I'm afraid of heights and if . . . *[ad-libs her way off stage]*

SCENE 3

Setting: A simple medical office with a small desk, two chairs, etc. Doctor Speck and Wilma are in his office sharing a final consultation.

DR. SPECK: Wilma, I'm sorry. I wish I had better news.

WILMA: Just tell me how much time, Doc.

DR. SPECK: Oh, a few months, maybe. You need to get things in order, Wilma. Have you told your family?

WILMA: *[with soft confidence]* Hey, Doc, it's okay. I have a guarantee for the hereafter. I am all set. *[pulls contract out of her purse and waves it]*

DR. SPECK: Wait a minute, Wilma. May I see that?

WILMA: Sure, Doc. I know some of my friends don't like this, but it is the only hope I have.

DR. SPECK: *[looking at contract]* Wilma, have you read the fine print?

WILMA: Sure have, Doc. No big deal. It's that Greek and Hebrew . . . you know, Eternal Life talk that says this is the real thing.

DR. SPECK: Wilma, it is Latin, and it means this contract is only good as long as you live. It is no good after you die.

WILMA: But, Doc, I paid good money to guarantee . . .

DR. SPECK: Wilma, there are no guarantees. No one can promise you life in the here-after.

WILMA: Then we have no hope.

DR. SPECK: Rather miserable isn't it, Wilma?

8

God Doesn't Give Up

THEME

Many times we feel that God has forgotten us or given up on us because of our sinful choices. However, God does not leave us nor forsake us. Yes, sometimes He is rather quiet. But He knows when to speak and the best way to get our attention. That is what Adam and Eve discovered in the Garden.

CHARACTERS

ADAM: As in the first man. He is dressed in a plain-colored sweat suit.

EVE: As in the first man's wife. She is dressed similarly to Adam.

VOICE: As in the voice of God. It is kind and strong.

SETTING

The Garden of Eden is rather simple with a park bench and a few plants. A half-eaten apple is needed as a prop.

Adam and Eve are sitting on the park bench, not facing each other and not talking. They are kind of "putting themselves back together." Their hair is a bit messed, clothes wrinkled, etc. They look extremely guilty, embarrassed, and are looking around to make sure no one sees them.

EVE: *[looking around, very nervous]* I . . . I think we blew it.

ADAM: *[short pause]* I . . . think you're right . . . *[a bit vindictive]* for the first time.

EVE: *[angry]* And what is *that* supposed to mean?

ADAM: Nothing . . . just nothing.

EVE: *[fidgeting]* Do you think anyone saw us?

ADAM: I didn't see anyone around . . . but *[looks up]* you never know.

EVE: *[as Adam looks up, she does the same]* I'll bet *He* saw us. What do you think?

ADAM: I'm not sure. He doesn't miss much that goes on around here.

EVE: *[pauses . . . a bit upset]* Did you really think we could get away with this?

39

ADAM: *[a bit angry and defensive]* Me? Me? Look, this was all your idea. You're the one who wanted to do this, not me.

EVE: *[hurt and sarcastic]* Oh, I get it. Now this is all my fault.

ADAM: Bingo.

EVE: Okay, okay, I'll take the blame. I can see how this is going to go down.

ADAM: Look, let's just drop it. *[looks away in disgust, pauses]*

EVE: It wasn't that good, was it?

ADAM: Nope. . . . *[pulls out an apple with a couple of bites in it]* I thought it was kind of bitter, not sweet at all. I think we got schnookered.

EVE: So, what are we going to do?

ADAM: I don't know. Wait, I guess.

EVE: Wait for what?

ADAM: Wait to hear . . . *[looks up and points up]* what *He* has to say . . . or what *He* is going to do.

EVE: What time is it?

ADAM: I don't know. Do you have a watch?

EVE: No. . . . *[curious]* What is a watch?

ADAM: *[rolls eyes, gets up to leave]* I'll see ya later.

EVE: Wait a minute, you aren't leaving me now.

ADAM: *[pause]* Shhh. . . . Did you hear that? *[They nervously look around as Adam grabs Eve's arm.]*

EVE: Hear what?

ADAM: That noise.

EVE: No, what noise?

ADAM: There, . . . that noise. . . . I think it is—

EVE: The wind, Adam, it's the wind. *[pause]* How long has it been since, you know, we took the bite?

ADAM:	*[looks at watch]* About twenty-three hours.
EVE:	*[looks at watch]* What is that?
ADAM:	My new watch.
EVE:	Where did you get that?
ADAM:	K-Mart. *[Eve looks puzzled.]* And I am not taking you by the produce department after the fine mess you got us into.
EVE:	There you go again. *[they angrily fold their arms and sit back-to-back; pause]* He's not coming, is He?
ADAM:	I don't think so.
EVE:	I'm getting cold.
ADAM:	Me too. I could use a sweater.
EVE:	What's a sweater?
ADAM:	*[pause, listening]* Shhhh . . . there it is again.
EVE:	Adam, you are hearing things.
ADAM:	*[fearful]* No. He's coming.
ADAM:	*[look at each other, frantic, then begin to yell]* God, we are here!
EVE:	Over here on the bench!
ADAM/EVE:	*[yell in unison]* God, we are sorry! *[silent pause to listen; no response; they slump back]*
ADAM:	*[dejected]* Well, I guess that's it.
EVE:	Yeah, nice knowing you. *[They shake hands. Eve gets up to leave.]*
ADAM:	Where are you going to go?
EVE:	Well, it isn't like I can go to my mother's. How about you?
ADAM:	I don't know. I never thought I would have to deal with this. *[short pause]* Now I know why that tree was off-limits. It would have been easier if we had just dropped dead . . . instead of this dying inside. *[They both get up to leave in opposite directions.]*

VOICE: Adam, Eve! *[Adam and Eve stop.]* I want to talk to you. *[They scramble back to the bench and sit at attention.]*

ADAM/EVE: God, we are ready to listen!

9

Devotions

THEME

Every believer senses a personal need to spend some quiet time with God, to listen and to share the intimate areas of life. We are all easily distracted, however, by the simplest desires and issues, like sleep.

CHARACTERS

MABEL: In her bathrobe, and her hair is in curlers. She enjoys the latest in novels and TV shows.

VOICE: The compassionate and convicting voice of God.

SETTING

A soft chair, table, lamp, etc., creates a comfortable bedroom, den, or living room scene.

Mabel is reading a book. In fact, she is really into her book, using all kinds of gestures and verbal expressions. Soft background music can be playing.

MABEL: *[with great passion]* And so John took Jane into his arms . . . and they rode off into the sunset, across the prairie, through the river, around the bend, over the hill, into the canyon, above the divide, and out of the forest . . . together . . . forever and ever . . . the end. *[using a tissue to dry her tears]* Oh, that Angela VanSheldon is such a good writer. *[yawn]* Well, I better get some sleep. *[Stretching/yawning, she starts getting up off the couch.]*

VOICE: Excuse me!

MABEL: *[freaks out, hits the deck, and grabs her book as a weapon]* Who said that?

VOICE: I did.

MABEL: *[with great fear]* Listen, Mr. "I Did," I don't know who you are, but—

VOICE: Look, don't be afraid. I know you don't recognize my voice. It has been a while since we have talked.

MABEL: *[panicking]* I . . . I have an attack guard dog here. You better leave before he eats you alive.

VOICE: Mabel, I know you don't have a dog. And I am not going to harm you. I just want to talk.

MABEL: *[timid]* You do? About what?

VOICE: About . . . me . . . and you.

MABEL: *[suspect]* What about me?

VOICE: Well, I know that the last few months have been rather rough at work, and I know how you feel about David "dumping" you.

MABEL: *[amazed]* Boy, you don't miss a beat, do you?

VOICE: I try not to. . . .

MABEL: *[realizes who it is]* Wait a minute. . . . You are—

VOICE: That's me. So, you haven't forgotten me?

MABEL: *[twinge of guilt]* Well, not exactly. *[a bit of ambivalence]* I suppose You want me to read Your book now?

VOICE: What do you think?

MABEL: *[tries to be positive]* Okay . . . good idea. . . . I was just about ready to crack the leather here. . . . Ah, *[under her breath]* where is that Bible? . . . I put it here somewhere. . . . *[She scrambles around looking under the furniture.]*

VOICE: Look over there, on the other side.

MABEL: *[looks up]* Thanks . . . I think. . . . Okay, I'm ready. . . .

VOICE: So am I. . . .

MABEL: I see . . . ah, You want me to open and read . . . Okay . . . *[Eyes closed, she opens to the middle, points with her finger at random, and begins to read.]* "Now when seventy years are completed for Babylon" . . . You know, this stuff just doesn't apply to me.

VOICE: What seems to be the problem?

MABEL: Well, first of all, I have never been to Babylon, and I am not seventy years old. Now I know why You call this the Old Testament.

VOICE: *[humored]* Keep reading.

MABEL:	All right. "I will come to you and fulfill my gracious promise to bring you back to this place."
VOICE:	So, what do you think?
MABEL:	Well, that is better . . . the part about *You* keeping *Your* promises.
VOICE:	I knew that would make you happy. . . . Go on.
MABEL:	"For I know the plans I have for you, plans to prosper you and not to harm you, plans to give you a hope and a future." I have a question about that.
VOICE:	Great! I thought you would never ask.
MABEL:	Now, about the future. Why can't You just tell me what is going to happen, instead of all of this cloak-and-dagger guessing-game stuff?
VOICE:	Wait a minute. Remember when I told you what would happen if you disobeyed me?
MABEL:	Okay, that time You were right on.
VOICE:	And remember—
MABEL:	Okay . . . I got the point. I need to trust You, right?
VOICE:	Bingo.
MABEL:	*[shocked]* Bingo? *[pleased]* Oh yeah, Bingo! Whew! Do You want me to keep going?
VOICE:	Only if you are ready for more.
MABEL:	No offense, but can I think about this stuff for a while?
VOICE:	Sure. When can we talk again? I have really enjoyed this time with you.
MABEL:	You have?
VOICE:	Yes, *[convincingly]* I have!
MABEL:	Great! Ah, I mean praise the Lord. . . . Or, praise *You!* See You in the morning.
VOICE:	I'll be there.

[Mabel holds Bible close and walks off with a smile.]

10

I Know She Is Coming. She Promised

THEME

We all have faith. But where do we place our faith? The answer to the question is different for almost every person. In this sketch, faith is placed in people during a crisis. Obviously, people let us down. Faithlessness comes out of misplaced faith.

CHARACTERS

DOREEN: Very nervous and dependent upon other people. She is going through a crisis. She finds that her friend, who has promised to be faithful, lets her down and destroys her trust again. She is dressed casually in scene 1 and wears a dress in scene 2.

MARSHA: Doreen's friend who simply forgot her appointment with Doreen. She is dressed casually in scene 1 and wears a dress in scene 2.

WAITRESS: A kind but streetwise "Rosanne" type of person. She is wearing a waitress uniform.

BUD: Marsha's friend. He wears dress slacks and shirt.

SETTING

Scene 1: Two chairs and two phones at the far ends of stage right and left. Side tables are optional.

Scene 2: A small decorated luncheon table with two chairs at stage center.

SCENE 1

Doreen and Marsha are seated on each side of the platform, talking to each other on the phone.

MARSHA: *[filing her nails at the same time, carefree]* Doreen, I know exactly what you are going through.

DOREEN: *[looking desperate and worried]* Oh, Marsha, I knew you would understand. . . .

MARSHA: Like I said, been there, done that.

DOREEN: Then do you think you can help me?

MARSHA: Piece of cake, Doreen. Now don't you worry about a thing. Hey, that's what friends are for.

DOREEN: And you are such a good friend.

MARSHA: I'm the best! Doreen, you can count on me.

DOREEN: Then you will meet me tomorrow for dinner?

MARSHA: Honey, you are in the schedule, on the calendar, and I am just going to help you through this, now don't you worry.

DOREEN: I could never get through this without you.

MARSHA: You've got it, babe!

DOREEN: Now, let me get this right, we are meeting at the Pine Street Café, on . . .

MARSHA: . . . Pine Street, dear, it is still on Pine Street.

DOREEN: And six o'clock is okay with you?

MARSHA: I'll be there.

DOREEN: Are you sure? You don't need a ride?

MARSHA: I'll be there.

DOREEN: [firm] Six o'clock at the Pine Street Café.

SCENE 2

Soft background music is played as Doreen is sitting at a table at the Pine Street Café. It appears that she has been sitting for quite some time. She is repeatedly looking at her watch, looking around the restaurant, and sipping her coffee.

WAITRESS: [walks up to Doreen with a pot of coffee in hand, chews gum] Would you like some more coffee?

DOREEN: No, well, what do you think? I've had four already.

WAITRESS: Honey, that is your fifth pot of coffee.

DOREEN: [apologetic] I feel like I've been here forever.

WAITRESS: You're close.

DOREEN: You haven't seen—

WAITRESS: No, dear, your best friend with _____ colored hair, about _____ feet _____ inches tall, who usually wears a _____ [color] dress, and goes by the name of Marsha. Nope, haven't seen her.

DOREEN: I guess I already asked, didn't I?

WAITRESS: *[looks at pad]* Seventeen and that makes it *[writes on pad]* eighteen times. But it's okay, I'm here to serve. Can I take your order?

DOREEN: Can you wait just a little longer?

WAITRESS: Why not? But let me take your dinner menu and get you a breakfast menu first.

DOREEN: I know that I have been waiting awhile . . .

WAITRESS: *[looks at watch]* Three hours and seventeen minutes.

DOREEN: Is it really?

WAITRESS: It's almost 9:30, dear. Why don't you give up on this Marsha?

DOREEN: *[musters some confidence]* Why, she is my best friend and . . . well . . . she made a promise that she would come and be here with me.

WAITRESS: Well, good luck, honey . . . but don't wait too long. Promises were made to be broken, but hearts break a whole lot easier.

[Marsha walks in.]

DOREEN: Well, thank you for your advice . . . *[yells]* Marsha!

WAITRESS: Well, I'll be . . . *[exits]*

MARSHA: *[surprised, looks around]* Doreen?

DOREEN: I knew you would come!

MARSHA: *[stammers]* Ah, Doreen, what are you . . . what a pleasant . . . day, no awful day . . . ah . . . this is Saturday.

DOREEN: *[kindly]* Listen, don't apologize for being a . . . little late. I just got here myself and was about to have a cup of coffee. . . .

MARSHA: A cup of coffee? *[sits in extra chair]*

DOREEN: Well, I have so much to talk to you about, I hope you have plenty of time.

[Bud enters and walks straight to Marsha.]

BUD: *[very casual and upbeat]* Marsha, there you are. . . . Ah, who is your friend?

MARSHA: Ah, Bud, this is Doreen. She is an old friend of mine.

DOREEN: *[to Bud]* Nice to meet you. *[to Marsha]* Now, as I was saying, I hope you have plenty of time . . .

BUD: Speaking of time, Marsha, our table is ready.

MARSHA: *[a bit embarrassed]* Thanks, Bud. I'll be right with you, Bud. *[gives him a nonverbal gesture to get lost]*

BUD: Yeah, well, don't make it too long. I'm starved.

DOREEN: *[figures things out]* Wait a minute . . . Marsha, you aren't here to see me, you are here with Bud and—

MARSHA: Doreen, let me explain . . .

DOREEN: *[angry]* Save it, Marsha, I don't need an explanation, things are very clear. *[searching for words]* Ah, . . . promises are made to be broken and so are hearts. So thank you, Marsha. *[leaving]* I hope you have a nice evening with Bud.

MARSHA: Doreen, we can do this tomorrow . . . I promise!

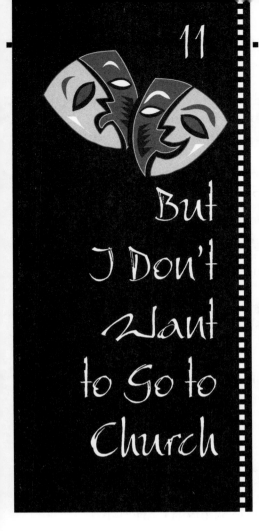

11

But I Don't Want to Go to Church

THEME

We all have two sides to our personality, one side that is public and the other that is private. It doesn't take long for those closest to us to pick up on this form of hypocrisy.

CHARACTERS

SARAH JEAN: A young teen who can be darling and not-so-darling. She wears a frilly dress.

ANNA MAY: Sarah Jean's mother. She has Southern charm and her image to protect. She wears Sunday-best clothes.

BETTY LOU: A new Christian who is out to discover all of the wonderful things of the Christian life. She is dressed semi-casually.

SETTING

Scene 1: Sarah Jean's bedroom with a small desk and chair at stage right.

Scene 2: A church pew or several chairs in a row at stage left.

SCENE 1

Sarah Jean is sitting at her desk, curling her hair. Anna May is off stage yelling at Sarah Jean. They are trying to get ready for church.

ANNA MAY: Sarah Jean, are you just about ready?

SARAH JEAN: *[apathetic]* Yes, Momma . . . but I don't want to go.

ANNA MAY: *[horrified]* What? What did my pure ears just hear? Oh my good La-wd, I am just going to pretend that I did not hear that less-than-angelic comment.

SARAH JEAN: Well, Momma, what's the point . . . going never does anybody any good. And how come Daddy doesn't have to go? He gets to go fishing and golfing and—

ANNA MAY: *[overly dramatic]* And this is what I get after *years* of sacrifice and hardship and trying so hard to be such a good and faithful Cha-ris-tian. You better change your attitude real fast, young lady, and start reflecting the joy of the Lawd, like me, your momma.

SARAH JEAN: Momma, think of all the fun stuff we could do if we just stayed home.

ANNA MAY: Sarah Jean, I can't believe those words are coming out of your Sunday-school-going, verse-quoting, song-singing mouth. I just hope and pray that the good Lawd does not strike you down, my first-born child, with such a promise.

SARAH JEAN: *[under her breath]* The only promise I'm making is to Billy Bob for the Friday night hayride.

ANNA MAY: What did you say, sweet child? I don't believe I heard you.

SARAH JEAN: Nothing Momma, just said it was a nice day for a ride.

ANNA MAY: *[comes out with hat, purse, gloves, ready to go, sugar sweet voice]* That is my girl. You make your momma proud. Now finish those last few curls so you can look your best at church.

[Sarah Jean has a look of pain, and Anna May looks proud as a peacock.]

SCENE 2

Church organ is playing and our mother/daughter duo comes in looking miserable and obviously not getting along.

ANNA MAY: You just sit right down there and make yourself look like a Christian. *[paints herself with a huge smile]*

SARAH JEAN: *[looking rather puzzled]* How would I know what one looks like, Momma. I'm not sure I have ever really seen one.

ANNA MAY: *[she raises her purse to strike Sarah Jean]* Well, the end of my purse will teach you about—*[Betty Lou approaches the pew. Anna May obviously sees her and quickly changes tone of her voice.]* . . . tithing. *[Quickly opens purse and takes out one dollar.]* We are going to be cheerful givers with happy and grateful attitudes to our Lawd.

BETTY LOU: Excuse me, may I please sit here next to you?

ANNA MAY: *[syrupy]* Oh, I didn't see you there *[Sarah Jean looks confused, knowing her mother is lying]*, of course you may. I'm Anna May and this is my lovely young daughter Sarah Jean. *[fakes a smile]* And what is your name?

BETTY LOU: My name is Betty Lou, Betty Lou Hawkins. I've been coming to the church now for nearly four weeks, and I've noticed you and your daughter. You are so faithful and look so happy to be here.

ANNA MAY:	There is no place we would rather be. Isn't that right, Sarah Jean, my precious little lamb?
SARAH JEAN:	*[looking absolutely miserable]* Whatever you say, Momma.
ANNA MAY:	Sarah Jean has memorized all of the Sunday school verses and has never missed a Sunday morning. Why, she would be here seven days a week if we didn't encourage her to do other things.
BETTY LOU:	And your husband?
SARAH JEAN:	He is out golf—
ANNA MAY:	*[quickly puts hand over Sarah Jean's mouth]* Gallbladder . . . out with a gall bladder. *[fakes a whimper]* In fact, it took him home, God rest his soul, a little over a year now. I'm so sorry you will never meet the man of my life and a pillar in this church and community.
SARAH JEAN:	*[very direct]* Daddy is not going to like that, Momma.
ANNA MAY:	*[scrambling]* Her father was such a humble man. Sarah Jean is concerned that Daddy, God rest his soul, is looking down from heaven and feeling a bit embarrassed.
BETTY LOU:	I'm sure he was a wonderful husband and father. Well, I am brand new to this community and a brand new Christian. I gave my heart to the Lord at my father's funeral about two months ago. I never even visited a church before Daddy died. So, I am learning all about the Christian life. It is real exciting learning to read the Bible, pray, and learn new attitudes and everything else.
ANNA MAY:	Oh yes, we know just what you are talking about. I read my Bible every day, especially before coming here. A right heart is a happy heart.
SARAH JEAN:	Momma, I don't think I feel so good.
ANNA MAY:	Now, what could possibly be wrong, my child?
SARAH JEAN:	I think the hypocrisy is getting to me, Momma.
BETTY LOU:	Oh my, what is that?
ANNA MAY:	Hiccups, a bad case of the hiccups. I guess we are going to have to leave.
BETTY LOU:	*[sincerely]* Well, I will be sure to pray for you.
ANNA MAY:	*[begins to soften]* You would? Why would you do that?

BETTY LOU: Well, I was reading in my Bible *[opens Bible]* that we need to pray for each other, especially if someone is not feeling well.

ANNA MAY: Really? The Bible says that?

BETTY LOU: Sure does, right here in the book of James.

ANNA MAY: *[interested]* No kidding, and you actually started doing that?

BETTY LOU: Not very well, but I am learning. I'm sure you can tell me a whole lot more . . . but just reading the Bible and watching fine Christian people has sure helped me change some of my lousy thinking. I had some bad attitudes. . . . Here is a great verse I read. . . .

[They begin looking through the Bible as the sketch fades out.]

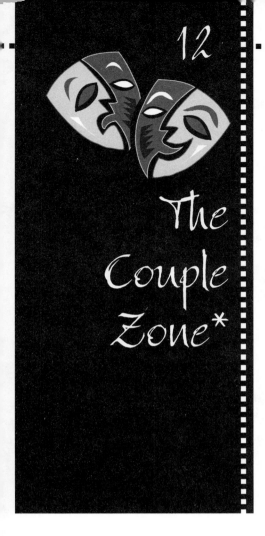

12

The Couple Zone*

THEME

Perfect families exist only in our minds. The first scene of this sketch reminds us that our dream of the perfect family is a bit of a joke. The second scene of this sketch brings us back to reality. It will not make us laugh. We will see ourselves, our parents, and our best friends.

CHARACTERS

BOB: Our everyday husband. He is wearing a shirt and tie. Props needed for scene 1 include a quart of milk and a rose.

ROBIN: Our everyday wife. She is dressed in Sunday best in scene 1, casual in scene 2.

ROD: (As in Serling) Our on-stage, deep-voiced, serious announcer.

SETTING

A typical dining/living room with a door, a table set for two with candles, and a couch with a newspaper.

*Sketch idea taken from "The Perfect Family," in *Sketch of the Week Club,* by Paul McCuster, August 1995.

SCENE 1

> *Music to* The Twilight Zone *begins. Bob walks to the door ready to open it, as Robin walks in the room to light the candles on the table. Both freeze. Rod walks on stage between them and begins his narration while the both remain frozen.*

ROD: *[slow, stoic, and very deliberate]* A fine line daily exists between fantasy and reality. A fantasy figment of incredible imagination lies at the heart and core of every marriage vow given at the flawless and faultless altar of everyone's wedding. Thus the journey begins in the world of fantasy, where everything is perfect and the honeymoon is never ending. Hopes, dreams, ideals, and the best of behavior are lived out as you will see in the perfect couple, Bob and Robin, in . . . *The Couple Zone. [Music continues as Rod walks offstage. Music stops and Bob and Robin come to life.]*

BOB: *[comes in carrying a carton of milk and a rose behind his back]* Sweetheart, love of my life, I am home.

ROBIN: *[lighting candles]* Oh, Bob, you are right on time, *[takes the milk]* and you got my message about the milk.

BOB: And for you, my dear. *[He drops to one knee and hands her the rose.]*

ROBIN: Another rose! That is the fifth one this week.

BOB: I guess I just lost count. Why, a garden of roses would not be enough for you, my love.

ROBIN: You are so thoughtful and so sweet. Now you just sit here *[walks him over to the couch and hands him a newspaper]* and read your newspaper while I put dinner on the table.

BOB: And what are those incredible, wonderful smells coming from your kitchen of culinary delights?

ROBIN: Liver and onions with leftover spinach.

BOB: So very healthy . . . and thrifty!

ROBIN: Not to mention savory and tasty!

BOB: Oh yes, and how can I help you, my dear?

ROBIN: *[a bit upset, she tries to mask her feelings]* It's okay, Bob, I have . . . everything . . . under control.

BOB: *[springs up from couch, moves toward her]* Wait a moment. I detect that something is troubling you. Sweetheart, we must talk and share these feelings. Is something wrong with the children?

ROBIN: No, Bob, the children are at the library doing research papers.

BOB: Is it our cat, Cuddles? She hasn't been hit by a—

ROBIN: *[forlorn]* Bob, it is . . . mother.

BOB: Mother? Oh, what can we do?

ROBIN: I think it will be okay, Bob. Her tomato plants were hit by a frost last night, but I am confident that they will survive. I hired a gardener to take care of everything.

BOB: Wise choice, my dear. I hope you will spare no expense on what we can do to help dear mother, the one who gave you birth and life and has brought me so much joy.

ROBIN: Bob, you are so good to us.

BOB: And you are to me, my love. *[pause]* Well, I sure am hungry.

ROBIN: And you should not wait a moment longer after your hard day at the office.

BOB: Then let me help you.

[They freeze. Music to The Twilight Zone *resumes. Rod comes walking out into the scene.]*

ROD: And so Bob will help Robin with a perfect dinner for the perfect couple. Their lives will go on uninterrupted by any real problems or real crises because Bob and Robin are not real. They represent the unrealistic expectations in everyone's imaginations, because they live in *The Couple Zone.*

[blackout; music gets louder; everyone exits stage]

SCENE 2

BOB: *[enters through the door; his hair is a mess, and his tie is half off; he is holding on to a newspaper like a weapon, and he yells:]* Robin! I'm home. *[flops on couch]* What's for dinner? I'm hungry.

ROBIN: *[comes out of kitchen carrying a frying pan like a weapon and yells:]* And I'm tired of you coming home for dinner every night asking, "What's for dinner?" You did pick up some milk, didn't you?

BOB: Hey look, I had a bad day at the office. So don't give me a bad time about the milk.

ROBIN: And I had a bad day with *your* daughter, so don't give me a bad time about no dinner.

BOB: You can't get anything right!

ROBIN: And you can't even get a quart of milk!

BOB: You can jump off a bridge.

ROBIN: And you can get your own dinner.

BOB: You know, there are some days when I would love to just—

ROBIN: Next time you come barking in here about no dinner, you can pack your bags and just—

BOB: Here we go again.

ROBIN: You never show any consideration for my feelings.

BOB: And you are always harping and griping about something.

ROBIN: You remind me of your father.

BOB: At least I'm not starting to look like your mother.

ROBIN: Oh, now you're getting dirty.

BOB: And you're starting to hit below the belt.

ROBIN: Well, there is plenty of reason to.

BOB: You just wait. I'll have you know that I just quit my job, and I can quit this marriage just as fast. *[swinging newspaper]* To the moon, Robin, to the moon.

ROBIN: Fine, and you can join your son and his friends. *[swinging frying pan]* Maybe you can catch him before he leaves town.

BOB/ROBIN: Ooooh, you make me so angry I could . . .

[Both freeze about ready to clobber each other with the newspaper and frying pan. Rod walks into the scene with the musical background from The Twilight Zone.*]*

ROD: *[very low key, but melodramatic]* What you have just witnessed is an American couple after a long day. Bob and Robin live in your neighborhood. They would love to kill each other. It is not a pretty sight, for you have just entered . . . reality.

[freeze; blackout; theme music changes to The Newlywed Show*]*

13

Success...
Only
a Dream

THEME

Many people have great hopes, aspirations, and dreams for success in their lives. The two characters in this sketch strive for financial success and political power, only to realize that all of those hopes and dreams are short-lived in light of eternity.

CHARACTERS

WILLIAM ADAMS: A flaming politician, who is well-groomed and dressed in a suit.

DONALD FORD: A high achieving businessman, who is well-groomed and dressed in a suit.

ANGEL: An angel dressed in white.

SETTING

Scene 1: Stage right: a desk, phone, and office chair. Stage left: a desk, phone, and office chair.

Scene 2: A four- or five-foot-wide panel at stage center, parallel with the audience provides a barrier and entrance for the two characters. A little smoke from a smoke machine would be ideal from behind the panel as scene 2 begins.

Director's Note: A smoke machine, and a sound effect of a crashing car would be great.

SCENE 1

William and Donald each sit at a desk on either side of the stage. They are on the phone, not talking to each other. Throughout scene 1, as one speaks the other freezes. Spotlight appears on one at a time.

DONALD: *[on the phone]* I have checked all of the financials and everything is in perfect order. You are going to be thrilled, JB, absolutely thrilled with my proposal. And need I say, you and I, *[coyly]* we, are all going to become very rich men. *[listening, responds very businesslike]* Uh-huh . . . of course . . . certainly. I have it covered. . . . Yes, I understand that we are taking a great risk. . . . Yes sir, I realize that everything is on the line. But you know this can only be a great success! *[freeze]*

WILLIAM: *[on the phone, reading a script]* Now listen to my final statement, "My fellow Americans, citizens and friends, we are embarking on a new frontier. If elected by the people, I will be for the people. Your vote can make a difference not only in your lifetime but in future generations. On this

Monday, you hold the key to the future. *[stands]* God bless you, everyone!" Well, what do you think? *[sits and listens, responds with a bit of insecurity]* You don't like the word embarking. . . . Okay, and what would you suggest? Yes, embracing is warmer than barking. Oh yes, I agree, my thoughts exactly. . . .You better believe I realize how important this speech is. Everything is riding on this speech. . . .Yes sir, I understand you are counting on me. I will make you proud. . . . I will not disappoint you, sir. . . . We will be in power and in control. You can count on this campaign being a great success! *[freeze]*

DONALD: Let me repeat those instructions: Third and Vine at the Embassy Towers, the third floor, suite 317, at . . . *[freeze]*

WILLIAM: Yes, sir, I will be at the Embassy Towers at the fifth floor ballroom at . . .

BOTH TOGETHER: One P.M. sharp. Yes, I know that this meeting means my career and our success. *I will not be late!*

[With parallel motion, both slam phone down, grab briefcases, and walk out behind center panel.]

SCENE 2

A loud crash is heard, smoke begins to billow out from behind the stage center panel. William and Donald enter from behind center panel. Both are totally disheveled and a bit dazed. They look like they have just been in the worst of accidents. As they pull themselves together and see one another, they lash out at each other.

DONALD: You! You ran a red light, you . . . you madman.

WILLIAM: It was as green as grass, you maniac.

DONALD: Maniac? Where did you learn to drive? At Girl Scouts?

WILLIAM: At least I learned, you monster on wheels.

DONALD: Do you even realize what this is going to cost me?

WILLIAM: Cost you? This is going to cost me a seat in the Senate.

DONALD: And I am losing millions of dollars because you ran a red light.

WILLIAM: Did not!

DONALD: Did too!

WILLIAM:	Did not!
DONALD:	Did!
WILLIAM:	Not!
DONALD:	Look, what time is it?
WILLIAM:	I don't know, you broke my watch in the accident.
BOTH TOGETHER:	Well, I have a one-o'clock appointment that is going to change my life.
DONALD:	*[to himself]* Well, say good-bye to being the next CEO of Megatronics.
WILLIAM:	*[to himself]* The senate and then the presidency is history, and now I won't be in the history books.
BOTH TOGETHER:	*[looking right at each other]* Thanks a lot, pal. You just ruined my life! *[Both sit down on the edge of the platform, head in hands. They pause. Donald looks toward William.]*
DONALD:	So, what do we do now?
WILLIAM:	I don't know. I never thought it would turn out like this.
DONALD:	Me either. My life was all charted out . . . even with its risks, and, as far as problems were concerned, . . .
WILLIAM:	Had a way to solve all those problems. Now there's no solution.
DONALD:	*[a voice of kindness]* Hey, can I buy you a cup of coffee?
WILLIAM:	*[kind response]* Sure, there's a little café around the corner. The owner is a good friend of mine.
DONALD:	*[grabs and opens wallet]* Huh? Sorry, bud, I'm out of cash.
WILLIAM:	And I don't think I'd be welcome in the café, now that I'm not going to be the next senator.
BOTH TOGETHER:	I sure did let a lot of people down.
	[Angel enters from behind the center panel, from where smoke is coming.]
ANGEL:	Donald and William?
BOTH TOGETHER:	Yeah, . . . that's me.

ANGEL: It is time for you to come.

DONALD: Come? Come where?

ANGEL: Just follow me.

WILLIAM: Wait a minute, we're not going anywhere unless you tell us where we are going.

ANGEL: I don't think you have a choice. . . .

DONALD: Look, you are looking at two very successful people, and we have a choice in life.

WILLIAM: Of course we have a choice, life is full of choices.

ANGEL: You are right, life *was* full of choices. But I am sorry, your lives are now over, and you've already made your choices. Now you will come with me.

[lights down; music plays; they all exit]

14

The Truth Is, We Are Lost!

THEME

God's truth is absolute. It is guaranteed, imperative truth that will never change or waiver. Human truth tends to be experiential, demanding proof with pragmatic results. Our voyagers in this sketch will test what is true and what is not.

CHARACTERS

HENRY: A nice, easygoing sort of person. He is honest and sincere in all of his relationships. He believes that his compass will help find the way to safety. He is wearing a life vest.

ALBERT: A tough, uncompromising, loudmouth who doesn't believe anything until he can see it and touch it. Albert is also wearing a life vest.

SETTING

A rubber life raft is stage center.

Both characters are seated at opposite ends of the life raft. They are in a freeze position: Albert shaking his finger at Henry, while Henry is looking at his watch. The music goes down as the light comes up. Then the action and dialogue begins.

ALBERT: *[angry]* Look, Henry, we are in this fine mess because of you and your stupid, idiotic decision to go fishing on Friday the thirteenth.

HENRY: *[apologetic]* I . . . I'm sorry, Albert, but I really thought it would be a good day.

ALBERT: Good day? Good grief is more like it! I don't call ten-foot waves and thunderstorms and a sinking boat a good day!

HENRY: *[trying to be optimistic]* Well, it is not raining now, and at least we have this life raft.

ALBERT: *[mocking]* It's not raining now. *[angry]* And now we are going to die at sea in this stupid life raft.

63

HENRY: I'm sorry about the boat, Albert. I didn't realize that the fuel gauge on the boat was broken.

ALBERT: *[clear and direct]* Henry, it wasn't the fuel gauge that got us here, it was the hole in the bottom of the boat that took in water that caused the boat to sink. And here we are without a hint of land in sight.

HENRY: *[a bit forlorn]* Yeah, it was a nice boat. I'm sorry about the leak.

ALBERT: *[bitter]* Sorry about the leak. *[louder]* Sorry about the fuel gauge. *[louder, in his face]* Sorry about the ten-foot waves. Sorry about the hole in the boat. You are a sorry lot, and I'm sorry we are going to die out here with seagulls and Moby Dick.

HENRY: *[naive]* Actually, Albert, there aren't any whales in this part of the ocean. . . . Um . . . but I think that *[shaking his watch]* we are going to be okay.

ALBERT: Going to be okay? Daniel Boone you are not. Now, how do you figure? *[picks up plastic bottle]* We are out of water. The sun is blistering hot. We haven't had any food for two days, and you say we are going to be okay. . . . Okay, how do you figure, Columbus?

HENRY: Well, my compass just started working again, and we are drifting toward land.

ALBERT: *[grabs Henry's arm to look at the compass]* This is a toy. It has a cartoon figure on the front. Henry, do I look like a reasonable man?

HENRY: Well, of course you do.

ALBERT: *[a sense of sincere pleading]* Do I have a family back home that I desperately want to see again?

HENRY: Yeah, your kids are like my kids.

ALBERT: Then why do you insist that I believe some silly, little, toy compass?

HENRY: Because it works, Albert. It really works. The arrow always points north. It has never let me down. The kids used it last week to go from the front yard to the back yard.

ALBERT: *[rather softly]* Stand up.

HENRY: What?

ALBERT: *[firmly]* I said, stand up.

HENRY: *[nervously]* Albert, it is not wise to stand up in a small water craft . . . especially in the middle of the ocean.

ALBERT: *[loudly]* Stand up, you half-wit! *[Henry carefully stands.]* Now, stretch out your arms. *[He slowly does so with great reluctance.]* Thank you. . . . There, you are finally doing something useful. Now hang on. *[Albert begins to blow on Henry.]*

HENRY: Albert, what are you doing?

ALBERT: *[speaks between huffs and puffs]* I'm doing something that is going to get us out of this mess that you got us into. Just stay there. You are the sail, and I am the wind.

HENRY: *[looking at watch]* But we are going the wrong direction. This is not going to work. You are trying to blow us against the waves. And, according to my Captain Marvel Super Hyper-Cross Scientific Trainer Compass, the waves will carry us to land. We just need to relax and go for the ride. Besides, what good is your huffing and my standing going to accomplish?

ALBERT: Go for the ride? And what good am I doing? Look, Robinson Crusoe, I am doing a whole lot more than you. You, I might point out, are doing nothing but going for a ride and looking at that stupid compass that doesn't even work. This ride is downhill, pal, and you are not going to like the sudden stop at the end.

HENRY: *[puts arms down and speaks confidently and firmly for the first time]* Now, wait a minute, Albert, this compass does work, and you better trust it.

ALBERT: Trust it? Where did you get that cheap thing?

HENRY Well . . . I , ah . . . I sent away for it.

ALBERT: *[sarcastic]* Yeah, and how many box tops did it take to get it?

HENRY: Only twenty-one, but it was worth it. I really love Post Toasted Crispy Flakes with extra sugar. . . . *[serious and back to reality]* But you can make fun all you want, Albert, this compass is going to get us home. *[sits back down in the boat]*

ALBERT: Henry, give it up. Face the music. We are goners, fish food, shark bait. It is you, me, and Captain Bly at the bottom of the sea.

HENRY: *[with absolute confidence]* Albert, the compass says we are going to be okay.

ALBERT: Henry, when I see the land, touch the land, and eat dirt, then I will believe in your toy compass. *[holds up bottle again]* In fact, I will eat a bottle of dirt if we ever get out of this mess.

HENRY: *[looks at his compass, looks out at the water several times to confirm his new discovery]* Albert?

ALBERT: *[leaning back on raft]* Yeah? What now?

HENRY: Albert, I would save that bottle. You're going to need it for your next meal. I think you call it "dirt in a bottle."

ALBERT: *[turns]* What?

[freeze]

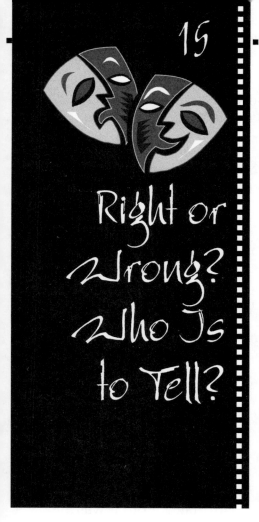

Right or Wrong? Who Is to Tell?

THEME

Each day people make decisions between right and wrong. That decision-making process includes listening to many voices. The voices come out of our past and present circumstances and the people in our lives. But what it often comes down to is the struggle between listening to God's Word or giving in to the tempting of the Evil One.

CHARACTERS

WILMA: On the outside she is kind and sweet and very gracious. On the inside she struggles with choices like everyone else. She is dressed semi-casually for shopping.

GOOD VOICE: Represents God's Word (dressed all in white).

BAD VOICE: Represents the temptation of the Enemy (dressed all in black).

SETTING

A clothes rack or two, with dresses hanging on them. A few signs would be helpful to create a dress shop.

Director's Note: Good Voice and Bad Voice constantly move on the stage with Wilma. They are her conscience, close by her side. Wilma does not address them directly.

Wilma comes walking into the dress shop. She seems to be happy and chipper. As she begins to look at the dresses, Bad Voice enters and moves to her side. Shortly after, Good Voice enters and moves to her other side.

WILMA: *[takes a dress out from the rack, models it in front of her]* Oh my, I can't believe I found it! This is the perfect dress. Fred is going to love it when I show up in this dress.

BAD VOICE: *[sneaks up to her from behind, with a smooth approach]* Ooo la la, look at you! That's right, Wilma. You will be the best-looking woman at the party.

WILMA: *I* will be the best-looking woman at the party. *[gives a look like "where did that thought come from?"]* Mmmmm?

BAD VOICE: Especially better than that Emily Van Show-Off.

WILMA: Oh that Emily had the gall last year to wear the same dress that I bought. Why, that five-foot-ten-inch, 120-pounder was no better looking in that dress than . . .

BAD VOICE: *[with a bit of a comic sneer]* That's right, Wilma. You have a right to be angry. You need to be . . . honest . . . and let that Emily have it.

[Good Voice enters and joins Wilma's side.]

WILMA: *[looks at the price tag on the dress she is holding]* Oh my goodness, this dress is $325. Fred is going to kill me.

GOOD VOICE: It is too expensive, Wilma. You don't have the money.

BAD VOICE: Don't listen to her. Besides, what's better, Wilma? Fred being a little upset or *knocking Emily dead* by being the best-dressed woman at the party? Fred will get over it.

WILMA: Oh, . . . Fred will get over it. *[admiring the dress, with a look of fear at the price tag]* I am going to be . . . gorgeous!

GOOD VOICE: Wilma, is one hour of pride worth driving a wedge between you and Fred? You know things have been tight financially since Fred's surgery.

WILMA: *[resigns to the truth]* Oh, I suppose this dress isn't worth it. . . . But it was a nice thought . . . for a moment. *[puts dress back on the rack]*

GOOD VOICE: Good for you, Wilma. Now you are making a good choice.

BAD VOICE: *[irate]* What do you mean that dress isn't worth it? What you are saying is *you* aren't worth it! What happened to self-respect? *[in her ear]* You *are* worth it. You *deserve* the dress. Now buy the dress!

WILMA: You know, *[admiring dress]* I *have* worked hard this year. I *have* cut corners. I *have* been a good wife. *[Her voice gets stronger and louder as she develops a sense of confidence.]* I served on the PTA. I chaired the YWCA, and I ran the ESPA. *[dramatic]* I have given, given, given. *[picks up dress again]* I *deserve* this dress!

GOOD VOICE: Wilma, listen to yourself, I, I, I. Wilma, you are only thinking of yourself. Don't forget what this dress is going to say to Fred, to Emily, and to the rest who will see exactly what you are doing.

WILMA: Oh, well, Emily Van Show-Off will probably see right through me.

BAD VOICE: *[strong]* No she won't. You'll put her in her place.

WILMA: But then again.

BAD VOICE:	*[forceful]* Make up your mind.
GOOD VOICE:	*[soft reminder]* Think of the others.
WILMA:	*[desperate]* Oh, I don't know what to do!
BAD VOICE:	Buy the dress.
GOOD VOICE:	Wilma, last year's dress will be just fine.
BAD VOICE:	The dress.
GOOD VOICE:	Think of Fred
BAD VOICE:	Think of Emily.
GOOD VOICE:	Yes, think *of* Emily.
WILMA:	Emily hurt me last year . . . really bad.
BAD VOICE:	*[proud]* That's my Wilma. . . . You go, girl.
GOOD VOICE:	But Emily needs friends, and you can be that friend. And you know, Emily needs to know Jesus. Will this dress help?
BAD VOICE:	*[to Good Voice]* Hey, *excuse* me, that was a low blow. Now we're bringing Jesus into this?
WILMA:	She does need Christ in her life.
BAD VOICE:	*[to Emily]* She needs to be taught a lesson. Don't let her push you around.
GOOD VOICE:	It is your choice, Wilma.
BAD VOICE:	There is no choice. Buy the dress.

[Wilma admires the dress and models it for a last time or two. She slowly puts the dress back on the rack.]

WILMA:	I love you, Fred. And . . . I . . . love you, Emily. Most of all, I love You, Jesus.
BAD VOICE:	Aghhh! *[exits with head in hands]*
GOOD VOICE:	You made the right choice. *[exits with a smile]*
WILMA:	Yes, last year's dress will still look just fine. *[exits with no dress, but with a smile]*

Stressed
to the
Max

THEME

Everyone experiences stress to one degree or another. Some have a greater capacity to handle stress. But will we really trust God to see us through our most difficult and stressful times?

CHARACTERS

MAX: A business executive trying to make everyone happy. He finds that he cannot. He is dressed in a business suit.

MRS. MAX: Strong and demanding. She is dressed casually.

MAX'S BOSS: Strong and demanding. He wears a business suit.

MAX'S BANKER: Strong and demanding. He wears a business suit.

MAX'S DAUGHTER: Gentle but has high expectations of her dad. She is dressed casually.

SETTING

A small desk with a phone and a chair are set stage center. A phone ring sound effect is helpful. Max sits at his desk, facing the audience. The other characters are positioned on stage behind him, with their backs to the audience, each with a phone.

MAX: *[on the phone]* Yes, Mr. Stern. Oh, yes, I understand, by six o'clock on your desk tonight. Yes, sir, you will have it. I know it is 5:01, *[looks at watch, being positive]* but that gives me fifty-nine minutes to finish the proposal. Good night, sir. *[hangs up]* I will never make it! Stern is asking for the impossible.

[phone rings] Max here. Yes, dear, I did not forget our dinner engagement. Yes, I know it's at six o'clock, but I don't know if— Hello? *[hangs up phone]* Oh, am I in the doghouse.

[phone rings] Hello? Hi, Cindy, how are you, honey? Your swim meet is tonight? But I thought you said it was tomorrow. It got moved? I see. *[with great hesitation]* I don't know if I can . . . *[wiping brow in despair]* Yes, I understand it begins at six-thirty. I know I promised. . . . I will see what I can do. I love you too, sweetheart. *[hangs up phone]* What a miserable father I am.

[phone rings] Hello? Ah, Mr. Tightwad? *[catches himself]* I . . . I mean, Mr. Titus! How are you and things down at the Family Friendly Bank? Yes, I realize that I am sixty days late, but my wife's surgery . . . and my daughter's braces . . . and, well, there wasn't a bonus this year. Things

have been really tight, but I will have it. *[pause]* Yes, I understand. *[downcast]* Yes, I know how to spell *foreclosure*: f-o-r-e-c— and yes, sir, I will take care of everything Monday morning. No sir, there is no part of that word I do not understand either. Thank you for calling. *[hangs up phone]* I can't believe this! How am I supposed to be in three places at one time and come up with money I don't have? *[looking upward, becomes very articulate]* God, you said you would not give me any more than I can handle. . . .

MRS. MAX: *[turns toward Max]* You better be home before six, Max, and don't forget to stop by the grocers.

BOSS: *[turns toward Max]* Max, I need that proposal on my desk by six o'clock, and don't be late or it is walking papers for you.

DAUGHTER: *[turns toward Max]* Daddy, you promised to be at my swim meet. It is the biggest of the season. See you at six-thirty.

BANKER: *[turns toward Max]* Your loan is sixty days past due and you have until Monday morning to come up with your payment.

MAX: What am I going to do? *[buries head in hands on desk]*

MRS. MAX: *[steps toward Max]* You better be home before six, Max.

BOSS: *[steps toward Max]* Max, I need that proposal on my desk by six.

DAUGHTER: *[steps toward Max]* Daddy, you promised to be at my six-thirty swim meet.

BANKER: *[steps toward Max]* You have until Monday morning or it is foreclosure time.

[Max looks around in desperation.]

MRS. MAX: *[steps toward Max again]* You better be home before six, Max.

BOSS: *[steps toward Max again]* Max, I need that proposal on my desk by six.

DAUGHTER: *[steps toward Max again]* Daddy, you promised to be at my six-thirty swim meet.

BANKER: *[steps toward Max again]* You have until Monday morning or it is foreclosure time.

[The next four lines are said at the same time, as they all take one giant step closer to Max at the same time.]

MRS. MAX: You better be home before six, Max.

BOSS: Max, I need that proposal on my desk by six.

DAUGHTER: Daddy, you promised to be at my six-thirty swim meet.

BANKER: You have until Monday morning or it is foreclosure time.

MAX: *[cries out]* Can't you understand? I can't, I can't, I can't do what you want me to do!

MRS. MAX: Six o'clock, Max!

BOSS: On my desk by six!

DAUGHTER: Swim meet is at six-thirty!

BANKER: Monday morning is the deadline!

[Each repeats above phrase louder and louder, and they all start talking at the same time.]

MAX: *[stands and yells]* Stop it! I can't take this anymore! *[Everyone freezes. Max looks up to God.]* All right . . . all right. . . . *[silence/pause]* You win. You are in control. And yes, I need some help. I know that I can't do this—*[looks around]* any of this—without . . . without You. *[very sober]* I give up. It is all Yours.

[The four characters slowly go back to their original place on stage, with their backs to the audience. They begin again, with much softer attitudes.]

MRS. MAX: *[turns toward Max, kind]* Max, I just wanted to let you know that the Tardy family can't make it for dinner tonight. Their youngest has chicken pox, so you won't need to stop by the store on your way home. *[positive]* See you when you get here! *[freeze]*

BOSS: *[turns toward Max, kind]* Max, don't worry about that proposal, we just had a major modification with the exchange commission. See you Monday morning. Oh, by the way, we will be handing out bonuses next week. So, have a nice weekend. *[freeze]*

DAUGHTER: *[turns toward Max, apologetic yet cheerful]* Daddy, it's me. I'm sorry, the meet is rescheduled for next week Saturday. Just a little mistake! I love you, bye! *[freeze]*

BANKER: *[turns toward Max, kind]* Max, Titus here . . . and don't say it, I know people call me "tightwad." Anyway, I can give you a couple of weeks, but try to send us what you can, Max. . . . We will work with you. *[freeze]*

MAX: *[slowly looks up]* I guess I really can trust You. Thanks. . . . *[pause]* Thanks . . . a lot.

[freeze; blackout]

THEME

Worship is an essential part of the believer's life in Christ. A new Christian begins a new adventure in worship. However, some people's definition of worship is different from others.

CHARACTERS

LARRY: A young man and a brand-new believer. His dress and appearance are very casual.

GRAHAM EDWARDS: An older man who has been in the church his entire life. He is dressed in a suit and tie and has every hair in place. He is as stuffy as his suit and is constantly annoyed by any distraction around him.

USHERS: Two men in suits who pass the collection plate.

SETTING

About four rows of chairs face stage front. Each row has about four chairs in it. A Bible and a hymnal are on every other chair.

Organ or piano plays an old familiar hymn. Graham walks in and takes a seat and stares forward. Larry comes in after him and tries to take a seat nearby.

GRAHAM: *[Just as Larry begins to sit down, he clears his throat.]* Hmm! *[cold and indifferent]* You would do well to try another place.

LARRY: *[confused, but polite]* Ah, thanks for the warning. Must be a broken seat, huh?

[Larry moves over to another row of chairs and begins to sit.]

GRAHAM: Those seats belong to the Fergusons, and I would not sit there if I were you.

LARRY: Whoa, people bring their own seats? Well, thanks for the warning.

[Larry moves over to another row and hears the same.]

GRAHAM: Hmm! Certainly not there either.

LARRY: The Fergusons?

GRAHAM: The Butterworths purchased those seats in 1909.

LARRY: Wow, do they still attend here?

GRAHAM: Their grandchildren are here every week.

[Larry tries another seat, and Graham simply gives a negative shake of the head. Graham reluctantly moves over and lets Larry sit next to him.]

LARRY: Ah, thanks, Mr. . . . . [extends hand] My name is Larry, and this is my first time here.

GRAHAM: No kidding. I would never have noticed had you not informed me.

LARRY: So, what is your name? And how long have you been coming?

GRAHAM: Graham, Graham Edwards. I was born in this church.

LARRY: No hospitals back then, huh? Well, Graham, do you have to work today?

GRAHAM: Of course not, this is the Sabbath, and I would never work on the Sabbath. What in the world would cause you to ask a question like that?

LARRY: Well, you are wearing a suit, and so . . . I thought you were a banker or something and were planning to go to work after the worship service. By the way, what is a Sabbath? I thought this was Sunday morning.

GRAHAM: [ignoring his comments] We are here to worship God . . . not work.

LARRY: Thanks for the clarification. [looking forward] What is happening now?

GRAHAM: We are beginning our worship and need to stand and sing the doxology.

LARRY: What is a [repeats with same inflections] doxology?

GRAHAM: It is how we begin our worship every week. Just sing.

LARRY: But I don't know the words.

GRAHAM: The hymn book, page 327.

LARRY: Wow, you have the songs memorized?

GRAHAM: Not that book, the other book. Don't you know the difference between a Bible and the hymnal?

LARRY: Well, as a matter of fact, I don't. Sorry. I'll try to get it right next time. They both kinda look the same.

GRAHAM: *[sits down]* The song is done. Would you please sit down? I cannot see the choir.

LARRY: Oh, sorry. *[listening]* Can you understand what they are singing?

GRAHAM: Of course, the words are familiar to all of us.

LARRY: I never heard them before, and with all those fancy parts it is just kind of hard to understand. Hey, what is an Ebenezer? They said they were going to raise their Ebenezer.

GRAHAM: Would you please be quiet? The Reverend is going to pray.

LARRY: Great, I love to pray. Are you going to pray next? Because if you do, I will be happy to go after you.

GRAHAM: Of course not. The Reverend prays, and we listen.

LARRY: So, we don't have to pray here? *[looks at Graham]*

GRAHAM: *[looks at Larry, first eye-to-eye connection between the two]* You are beginning to catch on.

[Ushers enter and pass the collection plate.]

LARRY: What do these men want?

GRAHAM: They are taking the offering.

LARRY: For what?

GRAHAM: For the church.

LARRY: To do what?

GRAHAM: To pay the Reverend and keep the church nice and send out missionaries.

LARRY: *[positive]* That's it? Well, how much are you going to give?

GRAHAM: I beg your pardon? That is between me and God.

LARRY: Well, I just thought that you, being a regular here, could give me an idea of where to start.

GRAHAM: Ten percent.

LARRY: Ten percent?

GRAHAM: Ten percent.

LARRY: Ten percent of what?

GRAHAM: Ten percent of your income.

LARRY: That's it?

GRAHAM: That is enough, young man.

LARRY: Wow, I was going to give everything I had and trust God to take care of me for the rest of the week. But . . . you sure make this easy. *[looks around, pause]* Hey, I just became a Christian two weeks ago. I have read the entire New Testament. What do you think about all those things in the book of Revelation?

GRAHAM: Ideas, images, and things we cannot understand. Now please, just listen to the Reverend.

LARRY: *[listens with a few verbal responses, shows some confusion, looks at watch]* Hey, what did you think of the words to that doxology thing? Those are pretty great, aren't they? *[starts singing]* Praise God from whom all blessings flow—

GRAHAM: Shhhhh! We need to be quiet in church.

LARRY: Quiet? Yeah, okay . . . like in a library. *[uncomfortable pause . . . sings a little softer]* Praise God from whom—*[Graham gives him a scowl.]* Quiet, right, I need to be quiet. *[long pause]*

GRAHAM: *[stands]* Well, it certainly has been an experience meeting you.

LARRY: Yeah, me too. Thanks for teaching me so much about "the Sabbath." Hey, I have one question.

GRAHAM: Of course you do.

LARRY: When do we worship God?

[freeze; blackout; music plays out with an old hymn]

18

I Taught You Everything I Know

THEME

We have all heard the phrase "Do as I say, not as I do." People in authority often use it as a catch-all phrase to excuse behavior they don't wish to be modeled. In raising a child, however, it just doesn't work. A child will imitate his or her parents for better or for worse.

CHARACTERS

RICHARD: An all-American man who plays by his own rules but expects others (especially his son) to live by another set of standards. He is dressed very casually.

JUSTIN: Richard's son. He is an older teen who is living by his own rules. He is dressed as casually as possible.

ELLEN/NARRATOR: Justin's mom and Richard's first wife. She sits on a stool, just offstage right. She is dressed in nice casual clothes.

SETTING

A stool for Ellen is placed just offstage right. A table with lots of junk food on it and two chairs are stage center.

Ellen is sitting on her stool, but the light is on center stage. Richard enters with a bag of potato chips in hand and takes a seat, looking at his watch. Justin enters looking rather disheveled.

RICHARD: *[sarcastic]* Well, well, well. Look what the wind blew in.

JUSTIN: *[smart mouth]* Hey, Richard, isn't it past your bedtime?

RICHARD: Obviously, you know what time it is . . . or what time it isn't.

JUSTIN: I suppose it is half past being grounded again.

RICHARD: Sit down, boy. *[Justin sits with an attitude.]* You were grounded for tonight and that obviously hasn't done any good.

JUSTIN: Does it ever do any good? Look, let's just call it a night, Dad.

RICHARD: Just blow in and blow out and pretend nothing is ever wrong.

JUSTIN: Hey, you taught me well.

RICHARD: Sass, sass, nothing but sass and disrespect.

JUSTIN: Give me a break.

RICHARD: I would love to give you a break right across your ever lovin'—

[freeze; lights fade down on the men and come up on Ellen]

ELLEN: Hello, my name is Ellen, Ellen Martin, and that is my son Justin. I was Richard's first wife. And yes, those two have done nothing but argue and fight their whole lives. Richard learned from his father and now teaches Justin to be everything they both hate. And Justin is right. He learned how to blow in and blow out from his father. Richard has always been a free spirit, doing just as he pleases, with little or no concern for others around him. So, he knows he really can't expect anything different from Justin.

[Lights go down on Ellen, and come back up on center stage.]

JUSTIN: *[angry]* Dad, what do you expect from me?

RICHARD: Just a little respect, boy.

JUSTIN: Yeah, well that goes both ways.

RICHARD: Where were you tonight?

JUSTIN: Where do you think?

RICHARD: I told you that girl was no good for you. Why, only God knows what you two have been doing all night.

JUSTIN: Well, Dad, you ought to know.

RICHARD: And just what is that supposed to mean?

[freeze; lights fade out on the men and come up on Ellen]

ELLEN: *[to Richard]* Nice try, Richard. *[to audience]* Richard knew exactly what Justin meant. Justin wasn't too old before he figured out why our wedding anniversary was less than the age of his birthday. Plus, he heard Richard and me fight all the time about his office girls and his female clients and late night meetings. No, Justin was well educated in the birds and bees before he ever knew there were birds and bees.

[Lights go down on Ellen and come back up on center stage.]

JUSTIN: Look, Dad, I am tired, and I am going to bed.

[Justin gets up to walk offstage left, and Richard jumps up to confront him nose to nose.]

RICHARD: Look, boy, I am tired of you and your attitude!

JUSTIN: Dad, you are just plain tired, period!

RICHARD: *[gently pushes Justin backward]* Good grief, boy, you smell like a brewery. How many times have I told you what would happen if I caught you drinking again?

JUSTIN: Well, let's see, that makes one thousand two hundred—

RICHARD: *[standing firm with hand out]* Give me the keys to the car.

JUSTIN: Fine, have your piece of junk . . . *[throws Richard keys]* with two new dents. Besides, my legs aren't broken. *[walks away]*

RICHARD: Where are you going? Don't you walk out on me like this.

JUSTIN: *[stops and turns]* Why not, Dad? Give me one reason why not.

[freeze; lights fade out on the men and come up on Ellen]

ELLEN: Well, Richard doesn't have a good reason, because "Richard the escape artist" has taught Justin how to escape from all of his problems. Richard walked out on his parents when he was seventeen. He walked out on me at age twenty-seven. He left his second wife at thirty-seven and quit more sales jobs than you or I have time to list. So, Justin knows well how to walk out on everyone and everything that goes wrong. Justin even walked out on me. *[saddened]* The problem is, the kid has no place to go. Again, just like his father, no place to go.

[Lights go down on Ellen and come back up on center stage.]

RICHARD: *[hurt]* Fine, go. . . . Do your own thing.

JUSTIN: *[strong]* Thanks, Dad, I will. And there are some things that I can do quite well, thank you very much.

RICHARD: And those might be . . .

JUSTIN: Well, I am a pretty good worker.

RICHARD: You mean at the hardware store?

JUSTIN: Yeah, and I am a pretty good salesman. I can sell just about anything down there.

RICHARD: Well, you should be able to. I taught you everything you know.

[freeze; keep light up on stage center as light comes up on stage right]

ELLEN: And no words have been more truly spoken.

[freeze; blackout]

19

Totally Forgiven

THEME

Forgiveness is not a common theme in our culture. When someone forgives another, it is often met with a degree of skepticism or doubt. Forgiveness always seems to have conditions attached, as we see in this sketch.

CHARACTERS

RHONDA: A rather tough woman who has never experienced total forgiveness. She is dressed casually and carries a large shoulder bag.

BETTY: Rhonda's previous neighbor. She thinks she has a handle on forgiveness, only to find out she really doesn't. She is dressed in business attire and carries a bag.

BYSTANDER: An eavesdropper who probably understands forgiveness better than anyone. She is dressed very casually.

VOICE-OVER: A female voice intended to sound like an airport lobby announcer.

SETTING

A row of about eight plain chairs to indicate an airport lobby.

Voice-over is heard while the various characters come in and take a seat in the row of chairs. The first to enter is Bystander, who begins reading a book, or knitting (or whatever). The second to enter is Rhonda, who sits at the opposite end of Bystander. The last to enter is Betty, who recognizes her neighbor Rhonda and takes a seat next to her.

VOICE-OVER: Please do not leave your luggage unattended at any time. If luggage remains unattended, airport security will remove it immediately. *[pause]* Final call for flight number 1234 now leaving for Syracuse, connecting to Albany.

BETTY: *[noticing Rhonda]* Rhonda? Rhonda Anderson, is that you?

RHONDA: *[a little bite in her voice]* In the flesh. And if it isn't Betty, my old neighbor?

BETTY: My goodness, how long has it been?

RHONDA: *[apathetic]* Long.

BETTY: *[trying to make conversation, yet with an air of condescension]* Now, tell me, are you still working at the Piggly Wiggly?

RHONDA: I am afraid so.

BETTY: *[prying]* So, what are you doing going on an airplane?

RHONDA: *[with a sharp bite in her voice]* You mean, how can Rhonda afford to go on an airplane, don't you?

BETTY: Well, that is not *exactly* what I meant.

RHONDA: Sure it is, but whatever. . . . If you can believe it, I am going to a managers' training course.

BETTY: *[trying to make up for blowing it, cheesy]* Congratulations! Oh, I am so happy for you. I knew you would amount to some—

RHONDA: Save it, Betty. *[awkward pause]* So, do you still live in Kincade Estates?

BETTY: *[a bit evasive]* Well, . . . yes . . . for the time being.

RHONDA: So, moving up to "bigger and better" again, huh?

BETTY: *[a little embarrassed]* Well, not exactly. My husband had an affair with another woman, and I am going to see my sister for a few weeks—just until we can get back together and patch things up between us.

RHONDA: *[rather amused]* Hey, join the sorority of throwaways. *[tries to give her a high five, but Betty doesn't quite know how to respond]* Give the ol' boy *[makes a fist]* one of these for me, would ya?

BETTY :   *[trying to act confident in herself]* Well, I am not bitter or angry or anything bothersome like that.

RHONDA: Ah, baloney. Men are jerks and always will be. Go ahead, yell, scream, say whatever is on your mind, and don't let the ol' boy off the hook. At least it will make you feel better.

BETTY: *[trying to be dignified]* Why, of course not! I will not lower myself to that kind of barbaric activity. I am just going to . . . to forgive . . . and let go of all of this hurt and pain, and work on rebuilding my marriage.

BYSTANDER: Now you are making sense.

[Rhonda and Betty look at Bystander, wondering where she is coming from.]

RHONDA: Forgive? No one forgives! That is out of fairy tales.

BYSTANDER: I don't think so.

BETTY: *[defensive]* Well, I can forgive.

RHONDA: Okay, for how long?

BETTY: Well, I believe that it was a one-time thing, and my husband and I can patch things up.

RHONDA: What planet are you coming from? It is never a "one-time" thing. Your husband probably has had an affair going on for years.

BETTY: *[thinking realistically]* Well, if *that* is true then, of course, I *cannot* forgive him.

RHONDA: Ha! Just like I said, no one really forgives. And if they do, it is totally conditional. I tried that forgiveness stuff with my ex and it only gave him license to keep cheating on me. Look, girl, go to court, get all you can out of the weasel, string the boy up, and get a new life.

BETTY: Do you really think I should?

BYSTANDER: *[rather firm, but kind]* Don't listen to her.

BETTY: *[leaning over to address Bystander, a bit angry]* Hey, what do you know about it?

BYSTANDER: I only know that I left my family several years ago, and no one forgave me, and I have been alone ever since.

RHONDA: See, you heard it, no one forgives.

BYSTANDER: But if they had, my life would be different.

[Betty grabs her bag and gets up to leave.]

RHONDA: So is your flight leaving?

BETTY: *[clear change of mind]* No, I don't think I will be going to my sister's.

RHONDA: *[still hard driving]* It's you or him, neighbor. *[louder]* He will ruin you!

BETTY: Maybe on the outside but not on the inside.

BYSTANDER: Go for it, Betty. God bless you. . . . You can forgive, it's a promise.

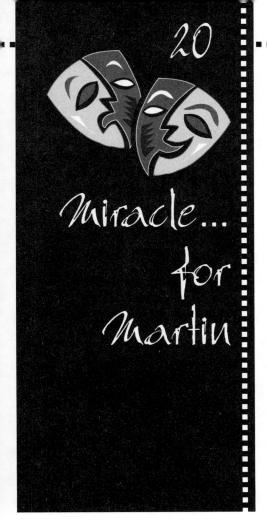

THEME

Everyone wants a miracle to happen in their lives. When a miracle happens in the life of another, however, we are often not so happy about it. Then, wrongfully, God does not get all the glory for what He does in people's lives.

CHARACTERS

EDGAR: An older gentleman in his seventies. He is dressed in pajamas and a robe.

EUGENE: Edgar's elderly friend. He is dressed the same.

SETTING

A hospital lounge with a couple of chairs or even wheelchairs.

Edgar slowly makes his way out to the chairs to begin reading his little book. Eugene joins him in short order.

EDGAR: *[less than cordial]* Hello, Eugene.

EUGENE: *[cordial]* Edgar. *[pauses to sit]* Do you have room for an old friend?

EDGAR: And what if I said "No?"

EUGENE: *[surprised]* Well, a good morning to you.

EDGAR: Whatever you say, Eugene. It is all a matter of perspective.

EUGENE: I know, you forgot to drink your prune juice this morning.

EDGAR: *[shrugs his shoulders, then says:]* These books are so stupid.

EUGENE: What's the problem, Einstein?

EDGAR: *[holds up book]* The good guy always wins. That is not real life, Eugene.

EUGENE: *[direct]* What is bugging you today?

EDGAR: *[in Eugene's face]* Martin!

EUGENE: Ha, I knew it wasn't the prune juice. So, what about Martin?

EDGAR: *[ticked]* He's gone.

EUGENE: Brilliant. I am going to recommend that you get a job with the FBI in the missing persons bureau.

EDGAR: *[looks Eugene straight in the eye, very serious]* He never said good-bye.

EUGENE: Well, now that you mention it . . .

EDGAR: And I was getting pretty sick of all those church people coming around.

EUGENE: Well, we finally agree on something.

EDGAR: All that praying and singing . . . for Martin to get healed . . . was driving me crazy.

EUGENE: Yeah, old Martin had more things wrong with his plumbing than the Titanic. Plus, I didn't know he even went to church.

EDGAR: He didn't. . . . That's one of my points. His kids stuck those church people on him. He hated church.

EUGENE: Go figure, Edgar. . . . Nothing makes sense these days.

EDGAR: Those people prayed too loud.

EUGENE: And too long! *[pause]* Well, do you think it worked?

EDGAR: Well, do you see him here?

EUGENE: Answer the question, Einstein.

EDGAR: Look, how do I know if it worked? *[bitter]* Martin never said good-bye.

EUGENE: You already said that.

EDGAR: Well, I really mean it. What kind of friend never says good-bye?

EUGENE: Well, you have a point, but, you know, I think you're jealous.

EDGAR: Jealous? Jealous of what?

EUGENE: Jealous that Martin had more things wrong with his plumbing than the state of New York, and he walked out of this dismal place . . . healed.

EDGAR: I ain't jealous.

EUGENE: Then what are you?

EDGAR: I am mad . . . mad that he never said good-bye.

EUGENE: That is the third time you have said that. You know very well what is wrong. You are mad that those church people didn't pray for *you,* and that Martin got healed and *you* didn't.

EDGAR: Am not.

EUGENE: You are too.

EDGAR: Am not!

EUGENE: *[strong]* Well, I am!

EDGAR: What did you say?

EUGENE: I am mad that they didn't pray for me. Martin got the miracle, and we didn't. He walked out of here, went back to his family, and we are stuck in this dismal state hospital.

EDGAR: So, why doesn't God do a miracle for you and me, like He did for Martin?

EUGENE: *[rather forlorn]* I guess God doesn't know we are here.

EDGAR: It is amazing to me how God does something special for a guy like Martin, and then "vamoose" . . . no more Martin. . . .

EUGENE: And no more miracles.

EDGAR: And no more church people coming around to pray . . . for us.

EUGENE: It is amazing.

EDGAR: *[pause]* Yup, amazing.

[Piano plays "Amazing Grace" as they exit.]

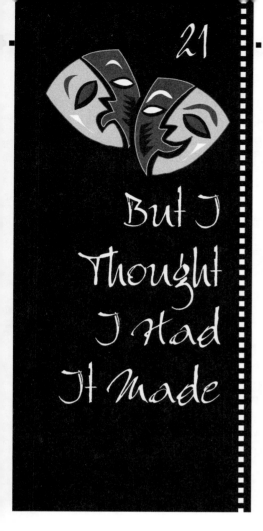

But I Thought I Had It Made

THEME

Many who were raised in a Christian or church background believe that going to church and doing everything "right" in God's name will guarantee them eternal life. On the other hand, those who have made simple commitments to Christ, often wonder or doubt their assurance to salvation as discovered in this sketch with a surprise ending.

CHARACTERS

JESSICA: The self-righteous church lady who seems to have all of the answers but finds that the biggest question cannot be answered correctly. She is dressed extremely conservatively, with a tad of "frump" (nothing matches). She is 15–30 years older than Angela.

ANGELA: She has obviously lived a rather difficult life. She has no confidence that she will inherit eternal life. She is dressed casually.

VOICE: Represents the voice of God.

SETTING

A waiting room with three chairs, end table, lamp, Bibles on table.

Music plays and Jessica comes walking out rather confident, singing a tune and checking everything out to pass inspection. She sits in the second chair. Angela follows a few moments later and simply goes straight to one of the available chairs next to Jessica. Angela walks without any confidence in her stride. Her head is down and her speech is very humble.

ANGELA: Excuse me, is this seat taken?

JESSICA: *[loud . . . overly friendly and very excited]* It's just you and me today, sweetie. You just go right ahead young lady and you take that seat. It has everything but your name written on it.

ANGELA: *[uncomfortable]* Thank you. Ah, are we supposed to check in or fill out any forms or anything?

JESSICA: *[laughs]* How would I know, sweetie? This is my first time here too. You only come here once, you know.

ANGELA: *[rather nervous]* That's true. . . . But, I sure wasn't planning on being here today. *[looking around]*

JESSICA: Neither was I, sweetie . . . neither was I. I don't think anyone really plans on being up here, but when our time comes it just comes. The final curtain has been pulled. Our number came up. And "pop" . . . goes that old weasel. But I am looking forward to my new place. I sure hope I can have pets . . . I always loved pets . . . down there; I was sure hoping they would be up here.

ANGELA: *[trying to be cordial]* Sure, ah . . . yeah . . . that would be nice.

JESSICA: *[looking Angela over very carefully]* Say, you look awfully familiar to me. Did you live in Freezeport?

ANGELA: Well, as a matter of fact, I did.

JESSICA: *[close in Angela's face]* Wait a minute, did you live in an older gray two-story on Walker street?

ANGELA: Yes, I did, *[looks carefully at Jessica, pauses]* . . . are you Mrs. Williams?

JESSICA: *[excited and stares back]* I'll be . . . and you are little Angela . . . the one who always got into troub . . . *[catches herself]* my how you have grown up.

ANGELA: I remember riding in your blue station wagon when we went to the city zoo every year.

JESSICA: Yes, yes . . . we were just being *kind and Christianly* to the neighbors . . . and we tried every week to get you to attend Sunday school, but you never wanted to come.

ANGELA: I did go once, but I ended up attending a Bible club at our school with one of my friends.

JESSICA: Well, I never missed a Sunday in church in the last eleven years. You'll hear about that real soon up here.

ANGELA: I am sure I will, Mrs. Williams.

JESSICA: And it would have been good if you had attended church yourself . . . I am sure you are worried how things will come out for you up here. Just remember, I did offer to bring you to church. . . . You can't say I never invited you.

ANGELA: Yes, ma'am, that is true . . . you called several times when I was little, before my dad left us.

JESSICA: That scoundrel of a father of yours was something else; whatever happened to that awful man?

ANGELA: I don't know, Mrs. Williams. I haven't seen or heard from Daddy in about eight years. I thought I might see him up here. *[looking around]*

JESSICA: *[preachy]* Not a chance, sweetie. The Good Book says that people reap what they sow!

ANGELA: Yes, ma'am, and our family had a lot of problems and so did I, but my best friend in the school Bible club taught me to pray and read my Bible and really seek after God when the days were long and discouraging . . . and I really sensed that when everyone else was gone, God was there.

JESSICA: Well, sweetie, you know where I was . . . I was in church! . . . with the sewing circle, the potlucks, children's choir, adult choir, and . . . the kitchen committee. . . . *[proudly]* I was busy, busy, busy serving the Lord and . . .

ANGELA: That's okay, Mrs. Williams. . . . I don't hold you responsible for anything.

JESSICA: *[offended and scolding]* Well, I should hope not. You know, if you had spent more time at our house instead of over at the Adams's house, you might not be in such a mess. I don't know what you saw in that naughty little Melissa Adams. She was a rascal.

ANGELA: Well, Melissa needed Jesus just like I did. . . . And even though I didn't have a nice house like you and Mr. Williams, I could be Melissa's friend and help her see that Jesus loved her like He loves me.

JESSICA: All of that love is good Angela, but you will soon see that the Good Book was right: "Bad company corrupts good morals" and "One bad apple spoils the whole basket" and, most of all, "God helps those who help themselves."

ANGELA: *[looks at Jessica a bit strangely]* But I really thought I was doing what was right . . . I guess I really blew it by not going to church like you.

JESSICA: Angela, God is good, and merciful and I am sure that He will give you a break, but you should have gone to church and gotten involved like the rest of us.

VOICE: Ladies, welcome. *[Both stand to their feet. Jessica is up quickly, and Angela stands very slow and humbly.]*

JESSICA: *[trying to be encouraging]* Oh, here we go . . . this is the Judgment Day! You better brace yourself. Now stand up and take what is coming to you, sweetie.

VOICE: Angela, you may remain seated.

JESSICA: *[looks at Angela, with passionate concern]* Oh sweetie, I knew this was going to happen to you. Listen, I will put in a good word for you . . . . I'll see what I can do. *[mellow dramatic piety]* Now, Lord, I hope it is okay to call You Lord, but this is Jessica Williams. I am sure You know me and my countless hours of service in Your church and my impeccable attendance at church, and I just want to offer one more good deed. This poor sweet girl . . .

VOICE: You mean Angela.

JESSICA: Yes, You are right. . . . Anyway, she has had a rough life, and even though she didn't ride with me to church each week, and even though she made some *horrible* decisions, I hope You will find it in Your *grace* and *mercy* to let her into a *heavenly home.*

VOICE: Angela, do you have anything to say for yourself?

ANGELA: Well, Lord, I want You to know that I love You, and even though I have messed up a lot, I did ask Jesus to have my whole life, and well, I am sure You were disappointed.

VOICE: Angela my daughter . . . I was disappointed on some days, but not enough to give up on you since you have simply trusted me. So, you will receive your full heavenly inheritance. Angela, through Melissa, I was thirsty and you gave me a drink, I was cold and you clothed me, I was hungry and you gave me to eat. So, well done good and faithful servant. *[Angela humbly bows her head].*

JESSICA: That was real nice of You, Lord. Now it is my turn.

VOICE: Oh yes, when I was hungry, you gave me nothing, when I was a stranger, you never invited me in . . .

JESSICA: But, Lord, my perfect attendance . . . didn't it count for something?

VOICE: Only the awards you received once a year at the church.

JESSICA: *[desperation]* Lord, what are You saying?

VOICE: Depart from me Mrs. Jessica Williams. . . . I never knew you! *[She looks up in fright.]*

[freeze; blackout]